X back

GREGG MICHAELSEN

Ex Back: Five Step Process to Get Him Back
Gregg Michaelsen

DISCLAIMER: As a male dating coach I am very good at what I do because of my years of studying the nuances of interpersonal relationships. I have helped thousands of women understand men.

That said, I am not a psychologist, doctor or licensed professional. So do not use my advice as a substitute if you need professional help.

TABLE of CONTENTS

Introduction

Welcome to the Five Step Process to Get Your Ex Back! While you may have read or at least perused the Five Steps on **WeCanGetYourExBack.com**, this book goes into more depth and includes a lot of content you won't find on the site.

Each step was carefully thought out and tested over several years and is proven to move you closer to getting your ex back. Within each step are activities to help you advance through that step and forward to the next. Each step is designed to build upon the previous steps and weave the entire process together seamlessly.

In **Step One**, you will learn to rein in your emotions. Right now, you want to curl up in a fetal position and listen to sad songs on your iPod or Alexa device repeatedly. You want to scream at your ex one minute and hug him the next. You're angry, you're sad, you're depressed, and you're overwhelmed by emotions.

It's scientifically proven that when you're experiencing this level of emotion, you're not able to use any sort of rational or logical thought processes and using logical thinking is necessary to get him back.

You'll learn how to implement the *No Contact Rule*, our way, and how to reel in your emotional mind while tapping into your rational mind so you can use more of what's known as your 'wise mind'. You'll learn what things you're doing to ruin your chances of getting him back and how to stop all the negative behaviors that you might be exhibiting. You'll also gain some tips on managing your anxiety and setting boundaries.

In **Step Two**, you will assess the relationship and breakup, take an honest look at what really happened, remove him from his pedestal and understand what he's thinking right now. You'll discover that he lied to you about why you broke up and what those lies really mean, and you'll learn the difference between missing him and missing someone. You will also identify your role in the breakup and uncover how you can fix that.

In **Step Three**, you will work on rebuilding your confidence. It doesn't matter what the reason for the breakup was; the result is a drop in your confidence. For your ex to want to be with you again, you need to rebuild that confidence. In this step, you'll learn what it means to be an independent woman and how to become one, why you need to make positive changes in your life and how to put them into practice, the importance of self-care and how to implement a self-care routine, and how to create a vision for your life and write your own story. You'll also learn how to stop living in the past and how to end the days of being a victim.

In **Step Four**, you'll have fun! You'll do what we call **toying with his psyche**. You'll start reminding him in small intermittent ways about the good times of your relationship. You'll learn about what I call the *Slip In/Slip Out* method and how to casually hang out. You'll determine when it's time to contact him and how all the things you'll be learning to do are going to turn the breakup upside down. He will question why he broke up with you and worry that he's losing you – not the other way around.

In the **final step**, you'll formulate your plan to meet your ex. You'll assess whether you're ready for this step and you'll learn how to get him to ask for the meeting. You'll also learn about how he is likely to act during this meeting and why. You will go into this meeting as a casual observer: kind, peaceful and calm, and he won't know what to do!

The first thing you'll learn, before those five steps, however, are the deal breakers. Pay close attention to these because these are all reasons why you should **not** consider a reconciliation with your ex. You might be afraid to read them, and that should be a big red flag that you need to!

This book is for every woman who is agonizing over her breakup right now and wishing her ex would knock on her door and take her back. We understand how you feel, and we are here to guide you through a process that provides you with the best possibility of getting him back, if you decide you still want him! Many women reach the end of Step Three and decide their ex is no longer worthy of them!

Either way, I encourage you to take your time through each step and read very carefully. If you don't rush, you'll have a better chance of having a fulfilling relationship when you complete this book! Whether that's with your ex or someone else is entirely up to you!

As a special thank you, and to help you on your quest to get your ex back, we want to offer you a free full-length book! *The Power to Communicate* was written to help everyone, male and female, improve their communication skills. It will help you learn how to detect different communication styles and respond accordingly. You'll learn how to listen effectively and you will gain the communication skills that will help you get anyone to do whatever it is you want them to do, simply by changing how you approach the situation.

Go to **whoholdsthecardsnow.com/ eb-free-power-to-communicate-sign-up** to get your free copy of this Amazon Best Seller today!

CHAPTER 1

Relationship Deal Breakers

There are some circumstances of your relationship that are deal breakers. In some situations, there isn't a relationship coach or therapist on the planet who will recommend that you get back together with your ex.

I know that might not be what you want to hear, but it is important for you to read this chapter to ensure that none of these apply to you.

DEAL BREAKER #1: Abuse and Anger Management Issues

If you were abused, either emotionally or physically by your ex, we will never encourage you to return to him. This type of person cannot change without extensive therapy. His simple promise to change, or his claim, after you've been gone for a couple days that he'll try to do better isn't enough.

There are underlying deep-seated issues with someone who feels that hitting another person or emotionally abusing them is okay. This person does this to you for reasons that have **nothing** to do with you. **Being abused by someone is not your fault.**

What is Physical Abuse?

Physical abuse occurs when someone intentionally causes harm to your body. It might not be a fist, it may be an object, like a belt or switch, or anything else that can cause harm. This contact causes you pain and suffering.

What is Emotional Abuse?

Emotional, or psychological abuse occurs when someone is gas-lighting you, bullying you and denying you your basic human rights. You should be able to move freely through your life without checking in or having trackers placed on your phone or vehicle, but when you're emotionally abused, you're often not granted these basic rights. Abusers choose if and where you will worship or work. It means you are enslaved or imprisoned and unable to freely live your life.

Gas-lighting is a key example of emotional abuse and refers to when someone says things that cause you to question your own perceptions or reality. The term comes from an old movie called Gaslight, in which a husband tricks his wife into believing she is insane so he can gain access to her money.

What Are Anger Management Issues?

Someone who has anger management issues can be harder to detect right away. This type of person may be able to keep their anger in check when they first meet you and may come off as being quite charming.

Then it will happen. Someone somewhere will push a button and BAM, this guy flies off the handle for something that seems to be rather small in comparison to his reaction. For example, if a waiter brought their meal out at a restaurant but forgot to leave the cheese off his hamburger as he requested. Instead of kindly asking for a remake, he blows up and starts calling the person names, yelling, and carrying on.

A person who is physically or emotionally abusing you has anger management issues, but not all people with anger management will appear to be abusive. It's possible that anger management issues only flare when alcohol is involved or when he's in a highly emotional situation and doesn't have the skills to navigate it.

Some folks with anger management issues turn it in on themselves and might self-harm or deny themselves things as punishment, but in an extreme way. For others, the anger management issues are outward expressions like yelling, breaking things or being physical.

Still others will use passive aggressive methods like sarcasm, speaking to others in a degrading way or giving someone the silent treatment.

Everyone experiences anger, but someone with anger management issues always feels angry and can regret his actions. Small petty actions can send them on an angry tirade.

In any of these three instances, your ex needs to want to change and seek help. Nothing with him will change unless he seeks therapy for these issues.

DEAL BREAKER #2: One or Both of You Abuse Drugs or Alcohol

If one or both of you are abusing drugs or alcohol, this is not the time to work on getting him back.

If he is the one who is abusing, he first must want to stop using and then, he needs to spend months in an environment designed to help him detox from the drugs or alcohol and address the underlying issues that caused the addiction.

Meanwhile, you would greatly benefit from attending therapy as well, and possibly joining an Alanon group to talk with other people who, like you, were held victim to an abuser.

If you are the one who is abusing drugs and/or alcohol, you need to want to stop using and then you need to avail yourself of an environment designed to help you detox and address the underlying issues relating to your addiction.

If your ex wants to get back with you, he will need to do the same therapy and Alanon recommended previously.

If it's both, you both must want to stop using to enter a new relationship together.

The power of addiction means it will be months, if not a year or more before either of you, regardless of who is the addict, are ready to get into a relationship again. Rushing the process will only lead to relapses and disappointment.

DEAL BREAKER #3: He Was NEVER There for You and/or He Was Selfish

In Step Two, you will do a better assessment of your relationship, but ask yourself this question right now.

In your darkest times while you were with your ex, was he there for you? Whether that meant he was a shoulder to cry on, a hand to hold, a soothing voice or a sounding board, was he there?

When you needed him, when things were tough, he should have been there for you, regardless of what you needed from him.

There are times when you need to rely on one another to carry a bigger load, to listen or to be the shoulder to cry on. If he wasn't that person for you before, he's not going to magically become that person in the future.

If he was only ever focused on his own needs, his own pleasure, or his own happiness, then he's a selfish individual who doesn't see your needs as being as important as his own.

Healthy relationships are about give and take. Sometimes one partner needs a little extra something from the other, but there will come a time when those roles will be reversed, and the actions should be reciprocated without malice or contempt.

If your guy wasn't there for you and didn't care much about what you needed, he's not going to change. His world only revolves around himself, and your needs are forever going to be secondary to his.

DEAL BREAKER #4: You Don't Have Enough History

Many people don't think of this one, but as you will see in Step Four, it's a crucial piece of the puzzle.

If you and your guy were only together for a few weeks, or even a few short months, you may not have enough history to woo him back.

Intimacy is built through spending time together, not by having sex. While people say they're getting intimate when they are trying to say they're having sex, the truth is that intimacy isn't built in bed. Think about any hookups you've had in the past. That was sex, but there was no intimacy.

Intimacy is built by going to cut down a Christmas tree together, by picking apples together, by learning to kayak together or going skiing for the first time together. It's built by surviving a storm together or going through something big, like the birth of a child, buying a new home together or having similar experiences.

Those moments, the memories, are fond memories for both of you and you will use those fond memories later to help him overcome the negative feelings he has toward you and your relationship right now.

But, if you haven't had the chance to build those memories, it makes it more difficult to get him to want to come back. The history just isn't there. Odds are he decided it wasn't working for him, and no matter how badly you thought it was working out, you weren't on the same page.

DEAL BREAKER #5: Your Opinion Doesn't Matter

When someone considers you their equal, they value your opinion. They don't need to agree with you, but they can at least allow you to have an opinion that may or may not differ from theirs.

This occurs in all aspects of your lives together. For example, if he never asks your opinion about where you're going to eat or what movie you'll see, he isn't valuing your opinion. And we are not referring to those instances where he says, *"Hey Babe, where would you like to go tonight?"* and you say, *"You decide,"* and he does. This is when he says, *"We're going to Charlie's for dinner tonight,"* or he blindsides you with, *"I took a promotion today. We're moving a thousand miles away in two weeks. Start packing."*

These big life decisions should be discussed between you. Obviously, if he wants to surprise you with a dinner out or a shiny new car, that's one thing, but never allowing you to voice your opinion means he doesn't see you as an equal partner in your relationship, and he won't be changing that any time soon.

DEAL BREAKER #6: Poor Hygiene

This is another one people often overlook but think about it. If someone doesn't even value themselves enough to shower regularly and take care of themselves, they can't place any value on you either and they lack respect for you.

Nobody wants to be with someone who smells badly and doesn't follow at least basic rules of hygiene. Of course, there are exceptions, such as someone whose mental health sometimes causes them to check out, but for most adults, this is not the case. In the case of mental health issues, he should be pursuing therapy for his issues so he can do better.

If he isn't doing so, you need to decide whether you want to stay. Someone who isn't willing to get help is getting something from poor mental health, be it attention or something similar. You don't owe this person anything so it's your choice.

DEAL BREAKER #7: Too High Maintenance

You might not think men can be high maintenance, but they can! While I was at the beach this past summer, I found myself next to such a man. He was clearly in his sixties, if not older, wearing a very skimpy Speedo swimsuit. At first, he was lying on his back getting a tan. Mind you, he was already tanned enough to rival a dark cup of coffee. After some time passed, I looked over and my jaw dropped to the sand. He had flipped over, pulled his swimsuit up so his butt was hanging out and was tanning his back side. This is a high maintenance man and it immediately made me wonder who he planned to impress with his tanned backside.

High maintenance people place a very high value on appearance over all else, which means he will also place a high value on your appearance. It could be he chose you because you were very attractive, very wealthy or had higher social status than he did. You add something to his overall appearance or status.

He will always be very focused on your appearance and his own, over other things of value like integrity, kindness, and decency.

If you want to work on yourself and improve your appearance, it should be because it's what you want, not what your partner is demanding of you. If you want to get liposuction, do it for yourself. If you want to start working out and buffing up your arms, go for it, but do it because it's what you want to do.

DEAL BREAKER #8: There Is No Long-Distance Exit Strategy

While many couples can exist in a long-distance relationship for quite some time, most couples have a plan for when they will live in the same city. Someone who refuses to make that plan with you or discuss a future life together in the same city probably doesn't see a long-term future for your relationship.

DEAL BREAKER #9: There Is No Chemistry

This happens a lot in relationships which begin online. You seem to have great chemistry while you're typing and texting away, but when you finally meet: Zero. Zip. Nada. No chemistry whatsoever.

Sometimes you believe if you hang in there for a while, it will come, and sometimes it will come, but if you've been together long enough to have a history together and there's no sexual chemistry, then it's not going to suddenly appear when you get back together.

Sexual chemistry isn't the same as sex, so if you aren't married and want to wait until you are to have sex, it doesn't mean there's no chemistry between you. The chemistry can still be there.

DEAL BREAKER #10: You Want and/or Believe in Different Things

Oftentimes, one of the biggest deal breakers is when you cannot agree on what you fundamentally want in life. The biggest thing that falls into this category is wanting or not wanting children. Some folks truly just don't want children and that's okay, but they should be in a relationship with someone else who doesn't want children. Be sure you know where you both stand on this important issue.

Other issues that may or may not be deal breakers, depending on your own values, include religion and politics.

It's possible for someone who is a Christian to be in a relationship with someone who isn't and it's possible for Democrats to be in relationships with Republicans, but you must agree to disagree and respect one another's choices on those matters.

DEAL BREAKER #11: Financial Irresponsibility or Stinginess

Financial responsibility allows you to live the life you want to live. It enables you to life stress-free and do things together. When one or both of you are financially irresponsible, you're adding layers of problems to your relationship.

If he's the one who is irresponsible, no amount of work on your part will change anything. The more you earn, the more irresponsible he will become. For him to be relationship material, he will need to learn to be more responsible.

If it's you, or both of you, your job is to take on becoming more responsible in your own financial life. Get your financial house in order. Learn how to budget and save. Pay down your debt and understand how finances work in areas like the stock market or crypto currencies.

On the flip side, there is such a thing as being too stingy. Someone who is too miserly isn't going to be any fun to be around. No matter how much extra is left over in the budget, he won't allow even a ten-dollar movie night.

There must be a balance between being too irresponsible and too miserly and you should be able to reach that together.

DEAL BREAKER #12: He Won't Work

If your guy is independently wealthy, great, then he may not need to work, but for the other ninety-nine percent of us, working is something that earns you that money you just read about.

A guy who would rather sit at home and play video games instead of earning an honest living is waving huge red flags.

There is a need within most men to be able to earn enough money to support their family. It's a point of pride for them. A man who doesn't have that drive is concerning.

And I'm not talking here about men who choose to be stay-at-home dads. Those guys earn medals as far as I'm concerned! That is a job and a full-time one at that!

If you're fine being the breadwinner while your man plays video games all day, go for it, but understand that he lacks the drive and determination to want to help support the household. This might not be a deal breaker for you, but you should at least give it some serious consideration.

DEAL BREAKER #13: The Workaholic

The flip side of the guy who won't work is the guy who works twenty-hour days, every day. What this says to you is that you aren't a priority in his life.

Oh sure, he might say he's doing it for you, but that's a lie. Being a workaholic means sacrificing the time and energy you would spend on other people in your life who should hold a place of importance.

Sometimes, people who are workaholics wake up and change, but others don't. Again, this isn't a deal breaker for everyone, but it's up to you to decide if you want to be with someone who would rather stare at his computer screen and count his bonus checks than to be with you.

DEAL BREAKER #14: You're a Secret

If you've been together long enough to have a history but you've never met his friends or family, something's very wrong, and it's most likely one of three things:

- He's married or in a committed relationship and you're the extra
- He's embarrassed by you in some way (his loss!)
- He can't commit

Any of these are deal breakers in themselves but when you find yourself a secret to everyone around him, it's time to run for the hills! Something is wrong.

DEAL BREAKER #15: He's Always Canceling Your Plans Together

You're dressed and ready for your date and you've texted to check on when he will be coming by to pick you up. One of two things happens next. Either he never replies, nor shows up, or he cancels your plans in favor of plans with someone or something else he claims was more important.

If he does this just once or twice, then this is okay, but when it begins to become the normal routine, it's a big signal that a larger problem lies beneath his excuses. It can be from the same list as Deal breaker #14 – he's married or he can't commit, or there could be another reason for it.

The fact is that if you're important enough in his life, his time with you will be important to him and he won't find reasons to cancel all the time.

DEAL BREAKER #16: You Just Know it in Your Gut

Your intuition is rarely wrong. If something inside you has been nudging you about this relationship, the chances are that you should listen to that.

When you spend time with your guy, you should feel good and happy. You shouldn't feel anxious (except perhaps on the first date of course) or stressed because you're about to see him. This is a signal that something isn't right.

It might be that he causes you to question your self-worth or maybe there is just something niggling at you that you can't quite identify. It is important that you listen to those inklings and cut your losses.

Next Steps

Now that you've assessed whether any of these deal breakers apply to you, it's time to make the decision to move in one direction or another.

I know it's tough to start out here and immediately recognize that while you really want your ex back, one of these deal breakers applies. You might still try to turn a blind eye to these deal breakers and try to get him back.

If you do, you will come to realize that it isn't meant to be. This might mean getting back with him and going through the same pain again, or you might discover it as you go through the first three steps of the process.

If you've already come to recognize that your relationship contains a deal breaker or two, you should still do the first three steps of the process because those are the steps that help you move forward in *any* relationship.

step 1

Getting Him Back: Rein in Your Emotions

It is impossible to think logically when you are overwhelmed with emotion, so the very first step you need to complete is to rein in your emotions. It's important to your thought process to overcome the highly emotional and maybe even angry state you're in now. Your emotional mind will override any logic that your rational mind might be trying to put forth. The result of this is impaired judgment, reactivity, and impulsiveness.

This first step is learning to understand how your own mind works. Anything you try to do to get your ex back while you're feeling this much emotion will only move you further from your goal.

Right now, your emotional mind and the stage of grieving the relationship that you're currently in are dictating your actions, which are likely to be reactive and impulsive. You act without thinking things through and you often blame those actions on someone else, probably your ex.

"He made me so angry…." The truth of being a human that many people never figure out is that you can and should learn to control your emotions. Nobody *makes* you angry, *you* make a choice, whether you realize it or not, to react to things in a specific way.

Many times, if you pause and count to ten, you will choose a reaction. It might be the same, but at least you chose it. You can still be angry, but now you can own it. *"I am so angry right now."* This indicates your control and your choice.

You'll learn the importance of moving forward with your life. I know that seems counter-intuitive, but that's what you need to do. The 'why behind this will become clearer as you read through the steps.

Each step builds on the tools you develop in the previous steps, so at the end of each step, you'll find a chapter that will help you evaluate your readiness to proceed. You will have measurable, actionable steps that you will be able to easily say *"Yep I did that"* or *"Nope, I still need to work on that"* and you can move on from there.

We have one goal and one goal only as you proceed through these steps and that is to provide you with the best skills possible to decide whether your ex is worthy of you, and whether you still want him back or whether he is simply not worthy of a wonderful woman like you, allowing you to move forward into life as a single woman on the hunt for a great guy who truly deserves you.

Don't panic when I say that. You will make that choice, and either way, nobody will judge you for it. You will make it based on being a confident woman who thinks with logic, passion, and reason. Many women come to the end of step three and decide their ex isn't worth chasing. Some women continue and get their guy back. And there are some instances in which the guy just doesn't want to come back.

I cannot predict which outcome you will have, but whatever it is, I can predict that you will be well prepared to move forward.

In Step One, you will learn the following:

- What the No Contact Rule is and why it's important, plus how to implement it
- The difference between your emotional mind, your rational mind, and your wise mind and how to tap into each properly
- The importance of avoiding the urge to retreat into yourself during this difficult time
- How to end the negative behaviors that are pushing him away, such as playing the blame game, being too needy, using desperation, begging, pity, angry outbursts and name calling, as well as trying to shower him with love and affection
- How to no longer be anyone's doormat
- That he will have a rebound relationship and the importance of your reaction to it
- The stages of grieving a relationship
- The best ways to alleviate your anxiety during this stressful time

CHAPTER 2

The No Contact Rule

What is the No Contact Rule?

The No Contact Rule is just what it sounds like. While your gut instincts are telling you to text him with your angry outbursts, your sadness and anything else, all in a desperate attempt to get him to come back, the truth is that it won't work. Ever.

Instead, it's time to stop contacting him. Of course, there are exceptions, like if you have kids together and need to talk about them, but in those instances, your conversation should stick to being about the kids and not your relationship. Otherwise, you need to stop texting him and leaving him voicemails.

But why does everyone talk about no contact? Why does it help and not hurt your chances of getting him back?

There are a few reasons, so let's dig into them now.

Why a No Contact Rule?

1. Neither of You Can Heal

The truth is that you need to heal. Yes, even if your goal is to get him back, you both need time for healing. Staying in contact while the wounds are fresh just keeps them open and doesn't allow any healing. It's like picking at a scab. Every time you do, it bleeds a little and hurts all over again.

Not only do you need to heal, but so does he, even if he's the one who initiated the breakup. He was either upset or angry enough to break things off and he needs time to process.

Men don't process emotions well. Most men aren't really raised to. They're raised to suck it up, man up, or stuff emotions. When your ex has emotions to deal with, and I guarantee you he has emotions to deal with, he needs to retreat. He's not like you and your girlfriends. Men don't have kumbaya moments where they all hug and talk about their feelings. They drink beer, watch football, and slap each other on the butts.

No, this doesn't promote healing, but he's able to get his mind off things and he will eventually retreat to his man cave to sort it all out.

2. It Forces You to Deal with Where You Are

I know you want him back, but that isn't where you are right now. That undertaking will soon come. Right now, you're broken up and to even think about getting back together, you must accept where you are right now.

You can't do that if you're constantly reaching out to him, whether he responds or not. If we assume for a moment that you do get him back, it will be a new relationship, not a continuation of the old one. Therefore, you need to deal with the end of that relationship.

You need to change your mindset, even if temporarily, to that of a single woman. By contacting him, you're staying stuck in the past and that won't help you move into the future.

3. It Puts an End to Co-Dependency

In a co-dependent relationship, you're more focused on the problems, feelings, needs and wants of your partner while ignoring your own.

You see the needs of your partner as being more important than your own. The time and energy you put into taking care of their needs takes away from your ability, time, and energy to take care of yourself. This is how you feel loved and worthwhile.

Instead, shift your focus to taking care of yourself. Spend time figuring out who you are, without relying on someone else to define that for you.

Co-dependent relationships are destined to fail, so if you had a co-dependent relationship previously, spend time now becoming an independent woman. This is the only way you can engage in healthy relationships in the future.

4. You Cut the Cord

Even if he broke up with you, he may still need this kick in the butt, a wakeup call of sorts. Some men will break up with you, but still want to keep you close by.

This is an unhealthy situation, and while it might make you think this means he wants to get back together, right now it doesn't. It just means he wants to keep his options open. He wants to be able to date other women and have you close at hand in case it doesn't work out.

He also needs to implement his own change. Your relationship together in the future won't work if neither of you make any changes. While you can't force him to change, you can give him the opportunity to do so. Right now, you both need space and that means no contact.

5. You End the Fantasy

Right after a breakup, you're more likely to recall, and even distort the good memories from your relationship. You're living in a fantasy world where there was nothing wrong and everything was rosy.

Contacting him keeps those fantasies alive and doesn't allow you to face the reality of your breakup. In Step Two, you'll assess the breakup and to do that, you need to take off those rose-colored glasses.

6. You can Stop Beating Yourself Up

If you aren't reliving the fantasy, chances are you're blaming yourself for everything, reliving every perceived mistake you made in the relationship and every flaw you believe you have.

This isn't productive either. You really want a do-over. You want to step back in time and recreate your history together, so he won't leave. Of course, this is unrealistic, unless you've created a time machine and not told anyone.

7. Remind Him He's Losing His "Stuff"

Please don't be upset at this one. Most women do not like to be called a man's stuff, but this is how men think, right or wrong, and men don't like to lose their stuff.

What he might be looking for right now is to be able to date around while still having you on the hook. You keep wanting him while he looks for someone else.

His plan is for you to sit and wallow, missing him and waiting for him to drag himself back to you, but you're not doing that, and this will shake him up a bit, in a good way.

He has no idea what is about to hit him!

How to Implement the No Contact Rule

The how is easy, in theory.

When you get the urge to reach out to him, stop. Don't text him, don't call him, don't message him on social media. Don't even like his stuff on social media. In fact, block his social media from yours.

I can hear you already, "But Gregg, I miss him, and I just want to say hello." I get it. I really do, but you can't, not right now.

If you find it difficult to stop reaching out to him, find something else to do when the urge strikes you. When you want to text him, redirect yourself to a hobby or binge watch something. Anything that distracts you from thinking about him will work.

Some women find adult coloring books to be a good distraction. Others throw themselves into home improvement projects or volunteering.

Get busy doing other things and you'll find your mind wanders to your ex much less.

What if He Contacts You?

This should probably be titled, what to do when he contacts you - because he will. I have no doubt about that. He will reach out, if for no other reason than he wants to keep you as a viable option just in case his plan to be single fails.

1. Wait a While to Reply

I know you'll be excited, blown away even, when he texts you, but you need to remain calm. Wait at least a few hours, if not a day, to reply.

This sends him a message that you aren't sitting around waiting to get some scrap from him. You're a busy woman and you're enjoying your life without him in it.

I understand that this might not be the case, but let's allow him to think it anyway.

2. Be Short and to The Point

He's grown accustomed to your long texts, so you're going to intrigue him with a short text that's direct and to the point. Providing a short response also sends a signal that you're too busy to sit there and craft a long message.

You're injecting mystery and challenge by not doing what he expects. In the past, he texted you and you ran to your phone to send him a reply right away.

Those days are over. When you get back together, you will continue both this and the last step. Men don't text in long paragraphs, which you probably already know, and they won't read them either. They text short messages that convey the point without being rude or condescending.

3. Make Him Believe You're Happy (Even if You Aren't)

It doesn't matter if you cry yourself to sleep every night, you want him to believe you're happy.

Guys don't like clingy and if you start in with how much you've missed him, he'll retreat again.

Instead, be quick and use lots of happy emojis or exclamation points. Maybe something like, "Hey, I'm out with the girls right now. Hope everything is good with you!!"

4. Be the One to End the Conversation

Politely let him know you need to keep moving because you're busy and have lots to do! You can try something like this, "Hey, I need to meet Susan for lunch. Maybe we can talk later."

He expects you to continue the conversation, but you're too busy. Again, this is injecting mystery and challenge. He's wondering how he can get back on your radar, so you'll want to talk to him again.

You're regaining power. You're giving yourself time to heal. You're allowing him time to miss you. The comeback is in the making.

5. Let Him Contact You Back

Letting him reach out to you tells him you aren't needy. You aren't sitting there pining away for him, wishing he would come back, even if you are.

Showing him that you're doing great and moving forward in your life is intriguing to him. It piques his interest and that's a good thing.

Sending him a message that you're unavailable creates a power shift from him to you. This is what you want!

Stay nice, be kind, but move away from his advances for now.

6. When He Contacts You by Phone

While most of these assume he's contacting you by text, it's possible he might contact you by phone. In that instance, be polite and allow him to lead the conversation. Make small talk and share some of the fun things you've been up to since he left. This shouldn't be a long conversation, though. Share a couple things and be done.

Be nice and cheery and be the one to end the call. Tell him you need to go - you have plans and mention that maybe you could talk again soon. Suggest a time for your conversation, have him call you, and end the call. Be aware he may or may not follow through but that's okay. You are laying the groundwork for him to capitulate in the future.

DO NOT mention your relationship, bring up past issues or your love life, try to make him jealous, say you're sorry, or start telling him how much you miss him. These are all like ticking bombs that will derail the conversation.

If he calls and wants to talk about the relationship, listen but seem indifferent. This is his call, and therefore he can do the talking.

Allow him to be intrigued by you, to shift the power to you, and to have him choose you, not vice versa.

Remember, you are building you while toying with him and it takes time. You need more time, and he needs more time if this is going to work. You **don't** want him back now because neither of you are ready.

Won't No Contact Make Him Move On?

If you're asking that question, you haven't accepted that your relationship is over. Unfortunately, the truth is that he broke up with you and that relationship has ended. I'm sorry to be so blunt, but it's the truth and the sooner you acknowledge it, the sooner you can work toward getting him back.

The answer to your question is no, no contact won't make him move on. One of the things he needs to do during this breakup is miss you, and if you're constantly texting him and leaving him voicemails, he doesn't get the chance to miss you. This means that any negative feelings he has toward you are validated.

Later, you will learn a powerful way in which you can contact him, but not until you're ready. This will ensure that he not only misses you but remembers the positive things about your relationship. *That* kind of contact is productive and works in your favor.

However, it's too soon for that now. He needs time to move past his negative feelings, and you need time to work through the first three steps.

I can't give you an exact time frame for using the contact methods you'll learn or for ending no contact. However, you will discover the tools as you proceed. Every person is different. You may move through this first step in just a day or two and then through the assessment of your relationship just as quickly.

Building your confidence is something that will come with time, but in order for it to be most effective, do so before you contact him. Step Three covers rebuilding your confidence – you cannot ignore this step!

You've probably already tried angry texts, begging texts, voicemails, and the like. Did those help get him back?

Of course not, so contacting him right now won't move you closer to getting him back. Radio silence is your best bet… for now.

CHAPTER 3

The Letter

Ideally, wait about one week after the No Contact Rule is in place before sending the letter. You don't want to wait too long after the breakup or it will just seem strange.

This short waiting period is important; it signals a shift in how you feel towards him, and it serves a purpose. It isn't representative of how you feel, but it is intended to trigger a reaction in him that his time is up, **he is losing you**.

You are encouraging the breakup.

In his mind, you're a mess without him. He's the only one who can satisfy you, but then he finds out this isn't the case, and he reacts.

You're turning the tables on him and playing him like he's playing you. Much of what you're learning are ploys men use against women. It's amazingly simple and effective!

How do You Write the Letter?

The letter needs to have a few critical elements.

It needs to be short, to the point, filled with a fond memory you shared, and you should use the word goodbye followed by his name. It's also best if it's hand-written.

> *"John, I just wanted to send a formal goodbye. Maybe for my own closure or maybe because I felt you deserved a better send off than how we ended it last week. I will miss apple picking with you at Brooksby Farm under our favorite tree (insert personal experience here) this autumn.*
>
> *Goodbye John,*
>
> *Carrie"*

Make the letter your own with a special memory of something he enjoyed doing with you. Don't go on and on; quick and to the point will do the job much better than pages and pages. Resist the urge to write more than a few short sentences.

The Keys to a Successful Letter

When you write your letter, keep these things in mind:

- He is expecting a novel, give him a paragraph, tops
- He expects desperation so keep that out of your letter
- He'll be shocked into recognizing that he is losing you
- He's reminded of an activity you both loved; if sex was part of it, even better
- He feels like you just broke up with him and that's a punch in the gut
- Close with Goodbye, which puts a lump in his throat; this is probably the first time he's heard those words coming at him instead of from him

It's Also About What You Don't Say

What you didn't say in this letter is as important as what you did say. You didn't berate him or ask for another chance. There is no begging or pleading for him to come back, no matter how much you want to say it. You never apologized.

Instead, you took his mind and gut and twisted them into a ball and lit them on fire!

Sometimes, a man will crawl back immediately after receiving the letter, but, read the next words carefully, **don't take the bait because your relationship will fail again**.

He's second-guessing the breakup, but that isn't the only thing you need to initiate a successful relationship. Nothing has changed for either of you. You're both the same people. One or both of you need to change or it will fail again.

What's He Thinking Now?

Now that he's received the letter, he needs time to process the idea of you dating someone new – of you having sex with someone else. As warped as this might sound to you, this is how a man's mind works when he loses or gives up his woman.

The thought of another man inside you is a very powerful and unpleasant feeling that he will face. This is what you want, and the letter expresses this in a very subtle way.

If he still loves you, this will work. For the first time in months or years, he realizes **you're also free to date others, not just him.**

He recalls how sexy you are and how great sex was with you and all the little quirky things about you that made him love you.

While he may have an epiphany, give him more time and do many more things for yourself before you consider taking him back. He still needs time to work through his own post-breakup thing.

How will He Respond?

He may respond soon after he receives the letter. There are few things for you to keep in mind:

- Be aloof – don't act like this response has changed your entire world – it hasn't
- Delay your response and any action you may offer him, *"Gee, Gregg, I'm busy this week, maybe next week"*
- Be kind

He will get the impression that you're okay with the breakup, or you're ready to date someone new. This is a good thing. I know it goes against what you believe will get him back, but trust the process that's helped thousands of women before you.

On the other hand, he might not respond at all. **Don't panic**!

It's okay if he doesn't respond. He might be angry and have residual contempt. He can't deal with the layer of emotion the letter brought on. His lack of response doesn't mean you didn't hit a nerve or tweak his feelings for you. **It doesn't mean there is no hope**.

In some cases, a man might not believe the letter. He ignores it and thinks, *"This can't be."*

He may reply and tell you he's happy and moving on. While this is hurtful, it's also not true. He is **not** moving on, but he wants you to think he is. Fine, let him toss around his lies.

Final Thoughts

- Do not send the letter as a text or email; hand-write it and send it through the mail
- Choose **one** memory that you know he is fond of, but **no more than one memory**
- Spritz a little of your perfume on the letter – smell is a powerful memory jogger
- Resist your urge to share dozens of memories and write pages and pages of stuff; he won't read it and you will have defeated your purpose in sending the letter
- Make no mention of the breakup, your feelings about it or anything negative
- The short paragraph will surprise him – he expects pages and pages of begging and apology; that isn't what he got…at all

This goes against everything you think you should do, and your response to what he does after he receives it does too, but trust the process.

CHAPTER 4

Emotional Mind vs. Rational Mind & Why It Matters

Within each of us are what we'll call three minds. There is an emotional mind, a rational mind, and a wise mind. Let's examine all three and uncover how to tap into your wise mind. You need it to make this work!

Your Emotional Mind

This is most likely you right now. When you operate strictly with your emotional mind, you're passionate, reactive, and impulsive. You're responding to gut feelings and moods.

This is not a time of logical or focused thinking. Your ability to evaluate facts and weigh options is curtailed. You may find it difficult to concentrate.

Your emotional mind is responsible for your desire to take risks or explore new territory.

It's exhausting to function just with your emotional mind. The erratic behavior and ever-changing whims will wear you out.

The emotional mind is not all bad. You draw from it when you start a new business or travel the world. Love comes from your emotional mind, and you certainly don't want to eliminate that!

Your Rational Mind

Your rational mind is cool and collected. It's logical, pragmatic, and methodical and you use it to make decisions like what degree to go after in college and where to live after.

Your rational mind deals with facts, and you're task oriented. If you need to stay focused and on target, you need your rational mind.

When you're trying to figure something out, tap into your rational mind. Use it for reading contracts, interpreting data, considering medical treatment and other similar activities.

Like the emotional mind, the rational mind has its pitfalls. Sometimes, people find so much comfort in their rational mind that they tend to hang out there. This causes them to come across as cool or aloof. It's challenging to develop an emotional connection with them.

Your Wise Mind

Your wise mind is the ideal place to be, most of the time. Your wise mind is intuitive, grounded, and balanced. It's the perfect balance between the rational mind and the emotional mind.

When you're using your wise mind, your heart and mind are working together, and the result is just what is needed. You control what you feel and how you express those feelings.

Your wise mind keeps you from missing those red flags that keep you from sleeping with a guy too soon. And it's the same mind that allows you to feel giddy and excited when you meet a new guy, driving you to want to spend more time with him.

Why is This Important?

To get your ex back you need your wise mind to be in control!

As you can see, being 100% in the emotional mind is not productive. While being passionate can be a good thing, it's not good when you aren't combining that passion with the good decision-making skills that come with your rational mind.

You also don't want to be operating at 100% rational mind either because this can lead you to come off as cold and impersonal.

The perfect marriage is to use both your emotional mind and your rational mind. This way, you get the best of both worlds!

How do You Get to Your Wise Mind?

This is an excellent question! It's easier than you think to begin using your wise mind.

To use your wise mind, practice mindfulness. Start to live more in the current moment and less in the past or future. Instead of judging your thoughts and feelings, or pushing them aside for later, allow them to pass on by.

It's okay to acknowledge thoughts that come through, such as anger, disappointment, sadness, and frustration, but you do so without judging yourself or those thoughts. You don't react to them; they simply pass through.

Imagine each thought is a leaf traveling down a stream. Watch them flow down the stream without touching them or judging them. Just watch them float by and give them a label – happy, angry, sad, frustrated, and so on.

Most of the time, we don't pay attention to our own thoughts. We think negative things about ourselves, but we never take time to say, *"Hey! That's not nice"* or *"That isn't really true."* Once you notice your thoughts, you can make changes.

Follow these steps to use your wise mind more often:

- Observe your thoughts without pushing them away; allow your thoughts to come and go, even when they're painful; give your thoughts and feelings a label – *"I feel really angry right now"*

- Describe what you're seeing or hearing without interpreting or judging; suppose someone walking by is wearing a skirt that you think is too short, instead of saying something like, *"That skirt is way too short for someone her age,"* you can simply say, *"That skirt is short"*
- Throw yourself into right now; don't focus on something that happened yesterday or even last week; don't worry about what might happen tomorrow; just live in this moment and fully experience it; instead of focusing on the old lady with the short skirt, look for the beauty of the landscape, the smell of flowers in the air or the gorgeous blue of the sky today
- Stick to observable facts instead of constantly inserting judgment; don't label everything as good or bad; just let it be - so the lady is in her sixties and her butt is hanging out of her skirt, just let it be, don't label it; and don't judge yourself when you discover you're judging, simply make a course correction
- Don't allow your emotions to control your behavior – this is called being reactive; when you say, *"That witch made me so mad when she cut me off,"* you're reactive; you can and should learn how to choose which emotion you want to use to react to something – take a moment to think about what you will say and curtail those negative emotions

Observe your thoughts and the rest will follow. Notice how much negativity comes out of your own mouth daily; it can be a real shock to the system. Each day, it will be less and less as you pay attention to it and make positive changes.

CHAPTER 5

The Nine Stages of Grieving a Relationship

Full Disclosure: This chapter is taken directly from my international best-seller, *He's Gone, Now What.* If you'd like to learn more about that book, check out **Recommended Reading** at the end of this book.

This chapter will help you heal so you can proceed through the steps to get your ex back. If you don't know what you are going through, it will hinder your recovery and you will lose time. You need to be strong again, fast!

Much like you grieve the loss of a loved one in death, you grieve the loss of a relationship. The phases are different, and they are not at all linear. You may recognize that you've gone in and out of some of them already. You may revisit some of them. That's normal.

Don't think you need to begin with the first one and progress through them straight to the end. There is no time frame in which you should complete each phase. You may stay in one for a day, a week, a month or even a year.

Shock

Shock will almost always be the first phase, based on how it presents. When you go through a breakup, several things happen rather suddenly:

- You discover you're replaceable in the heart of someone you thought would love you forever
- You suddenly feel irrelevant in his life
- You feel disposable
- You are no longer part of a couple – your identity changed
- Nobody checks up on you at night to make sure you got home okay
- The familiar sights, sounds, smells, touches and even tastes of your life are now different
- Your survival mode kicks in to compensate for the foggy, numb, spacey way you feel; your body shifts into autopilot

In the shock phase, a new reality kicks in immediately, forcing you to deal with a lot of altered chemical states and emotions which can make you feel uncomfortable in a multitude of ways.

Denial

In the denial phase, you tell yourself the breakup isn't real. He didn't mean the things he said. This isn't really happening, not to you. You can't imagine your life without him in it. You tell yourself he's going through a stage, or a phase and he'll be out of it soon, he'll come to his senses.

Your life continues as if you're still in the relationship. This is part of your primal response to the breakup. Your body is denying the withdrawal process. To keep those happy chemicals flowing, your mind is playing tricks and telling you things which, deep inside, you know are not true. You are postponing the grieving process to protect yourself from the pain.

You may not realize you're in denial. This is a subconscious response to the breakup, but, once you do realize you're in the denial phase, you must begin to recognize it as something different – avoidance.

Avoidance means you're avoiding facing the truth of the situation. You're avoiding the reality, because it means that you don't have to feel the pain.

Desperate For Answers

In this phase, you go on a full-on search for the *why* of the breakup. How did this happen to the two of you? Everything was perfect! You're not thinking logically in this phase.

This search for the why has a purpose, which is to disprove those 'hows' and 'whys'. All you need to do is show that the reasons for the breakup are not valid and everything will be okay again.

At some point, you conclude that there is no good reason for the breakup, so you fixate on why those reasons are no good. Your friends may quickly get tired of hanging out with you in this phase because you will tell anybody and everybody how irrational this breakup was. You state and restate all the reasons you've drummed up in your denial phase.

In all honesty, this phase is sort of a cushion. You're not yet ready to process the why. You are still in a place where you're avoiding the reality of the loss.

External Bargaining

In this phase, you get creative. If he will take you back, you'll do *anything*. You will singlehandedly fix everything that was wrong in the relationship. The relationship will be stronger and better than it ever was if he will just let you fix it.

Your ability to use your judgment and reasoning skills is significantly impaired during this phase. You aren't using your full ability to reason that you can't fix it all by yourself. The important question to ask is whether you are the only one at fault for the relationship ending. Would changing everything really solve all the problems in the relationship?

The truth, which you will discover at some point, is that one person cannot fix all the wrongs in any relationship. This would be an unreasonable burden to put on yourself, or him, but since you're still in a state of wanting to avoid or alleviate the pain of the breakup, you're not facing what you know to be true – you can't fix it by yourself.

Internal Bargaining

Have you heard yourself start a sentence with this: *"If only I had…"*?

Uh huh, I thought so. This is the typical sentence starter for the internal bargaining phase. In this phase, you internalize all the problems of the relationship. You envision different outcomes to all the problems of the relationship.

- *If only I had picked him up at the airport instead of making him take a cab*
- *If only I had kept up with the laundry*
- *If only I hadn't pushed him into buying that bigger house*

The reality is that those things didn't happen, and you can't go back in time to fix things. Much as we'd all like to, we can't change the past. The second half of this phase is that you can't guarantee that picking him up at the airport or doing the laundry in a timelier manner would have changed anything.

Relapse

It is possible that this breakup isn't the first for the two of you. You may have broken up and gotten back together once or twice before. This only feeds into this phase, which is the phase where you manage to convince him to reconcile with you.

This is yet another effort to alleviate the pain of the split and restart the flow of those happy chemicals your body craves. The problem is that the hurts from the past are still there, and they will rear their ugly heads sooner or later. Getting back together, especially if you've begged your way back in, is temporary at best. Neither of you has changed, nor have you likely given any real discussion to the problems of the relationship before the split.

You are not only avoiding the pain of the split, but you're avoiding the possibility of life after the split. You don't want to think about what your life might look like without him in it. That's too difficult to imagine at this point. This is yet another phase where you are delaying the pain of the breakup.

Initial Acceptance

Finally, right? You accept the breakup. You have moments of clarity when you see yourself living your life without him, but those moments of clarity are often mixed with irrational moments filled with elements of the other phases.

You will go in and out of initial acceptance a few times, especially early on. If you set yourself on a healthy healing course, your time in this phase will get longer and longer. You resist contacting him when you accept the breakup. Of course, in your relapse moments, you will fall again and probably reach out.

Over time, your successes will last longer. You will put boundaries in place which align with your values and help you see your life in the future instead of dwelling on the past.

Your first few times in the initial acceptance phase will be quick and you won't feel like you've gotten anywhere, but each time you come into this phase, you will find more success. It will build and build until you are able to get through it to another phase.

Anger

Anger takes many forms, depending on how soon after the breakup you're feeling it. In the beginning, you turn this anger on yourself. You look to your own shortcomings and blame yourself for what happened. You get angry with yourself for causing the breakup. Some nice negative self-talk can come in here. Stuff like:

- I'm too fat
- I'm too ugly
- I'm too stupid

In the anger phase, your main goal is to place blame. Venting anger is one way to do that. You'll know you've finally gotten over the anger phase when you realize you're angry over the breakup and no longer are trying to place blame.

The trick is to learn how to be responsible for your own anger. When you reach a point when you can do that, you will find that you are able to pull together the pieces of your life and move forward. This anger over the breakup gives you the energy to move forward.

Hope

Hope takes many forms during the process of grieving a relationship. In the early phase, hope takes the form of hoping you will get back together. You do anything and everything to revive the relationship.

Hopelessness is one of the worst emotions we can feel as humans. It is a truly desperate emotion. The only time human beings truly lose hope is when they are facing death. This means that, even in your worst feeling of hopelessness for the relationship, you can still access some sense of feeling hopeful instead.

As your grief progresses, your hope shifts from hoping the relationship can be saved to hoping you will survive without it. This shows a positive progression as you see your life without him in it.

As you get to that point, you build on your accomplishments. Each small thing you accomplish – each goal you reach or small victory you have in some area, will build into bigger and bigger accomplishments and victories.

What Does It Mean?

I have no doubt you can see yourself in several of these phases already. It is possible to be in more than one at a time and, as I said in the beginning, it is possible to come into and go out of these phases numerous times.

Don't beat yourself up if you get stuck in one phase or another for a while. Don't let your friends tell you that you need to move through these phases faster or that what you're feeling is silly or unnecessary. Each of these phases is necessary to move you through to a healthier, more confident woman.

What Can You Do?

Recognize that what you are experiencing is normal. Regardless of which phase you can most identify with right now, it's normal. Short of the shock phase, you won't go through these phases in the order they're presented here. You may skip some. You may stay in some phases for what seems to your friends and family to be too long. Kindly tell them that you need to process this in your own time, not theirs and keep plugging along.

Do the work inside this book, regardless of which phase you're in. Some of the work has obvious benefits to specific phases and some of the work hasn't even been presented to you yet. Where you are right now sucks, I know that. I also know that you might not feel like doing the work today. It may just feel too overwhelming -I get it. I'm not here to push you through a process you're not ready to go through. What I am here for is to be your coach, your guide. I am here to present to you the tools I know will help you.

I promise that you will feel better.

Don't wallow in self-pity, at least for very long. The whole *woe is me* thing won't get you anywhere. Feel it for a little while – allow yourself some specific amount of time, but never more than a few days at the most.

After you have done this, it is time to pick yourself up, dust yourself off and go find something to shift your energy and focus onto. There are days when you may not feel like getting out of bed but those are the days you're trying to get past. If you can't get out of bed, close your eyes, and visualize yourself doing something fun, like having lunch with a good friend or going out to buy a new pair of shoes. New shoes fix everything for women from what I understand.

Visualize a vacation you want to take or that new car you've been wanting to buy. Soon, the positive vibes from the visualization will motivate you out of your funk.

CHAPTER 6

These Negative Behaviors are Ruining Your Chances of Getting Him Back

Unfortunately, what your gut, your girlfriends, your mother, and your sisters are telling you to do right now is probably the exact opposite of what you should be doing.

Your mind is playing tricks on you to keep the love chemicals flowing. Depending on which stage of grieving the relationship you're in, there may be other factors driving negative behavior.

The good news is that you can control these behaviors and I know you will, once you understand what they are and how they're hurting your chances with your ex.

NEGATIVE BEHAVIOR #1: Freaking Out When He Dates Other Women

He will have a rebound relationship. I can almost guarantee it. I know you'll be upset, but what you cannot do is freak out about it. Know that this relationship for him is just that – a rebound. Most often, no long-term relationship comes from a rebound.

Meanwhile, your instincts and everyone around you is telling you he'll fall in love with this woman and your chances of getting back with him are over. They're wrong.

I've watched this movie play repeatedly. He dates someone who is the opposite of you. The pendulum swings too far. He thinks she is the answer, but she isn't. He loved you because of who you were. Yes, things changed, but you'll show him the woman he fell for in the beginning times ten.

His rebound relationship won't last.

NEGATIVE BEHAVIOR #2: Calling and Texting Him All the Time

These behaviors tell your ex you're needy and miserable without him. You're trying to convey that you miss him, but that isn't what he wants to hear, and it isn't really what you're saying either.

These texts are unattractive and indicate a lack of confidence. Instead of pulling him closer to you, they're pushing him further away.

NEGATIVE BEHAVIOR #3: Begging and Trying to use Pity to Win Him Back

He is expecting this, so the best thing you can do is *not do it.* Doing the opposite of what he expects sets him on his heels and makes him rethink the breakup. It's mysterious behavior because it's unexpected. Mysterious behavior is good.

This type of behavior makes you appear weak and insecure – i.e., a woman with no confidence.

No man will take you back because he pities you. No man worth having is attracted to this type of behavior or to someone who's miserable.

NEGATIVE BEHAVIOR #4: Showering Him with Love and Affection

If he can just *see* how much you love him, he'll come back, but he already knows how you feel, and it didn't change anything.

He still left and continuing this type of behavior will push him further away instead of closer.

NEGATIVE BEHAVIOR #5: Letting Him Walk All Over You

You are nobody's doormat. Not your ex, not your friends and not your boss. Doormats are *"Yes"* people. While it feels like you're being agreeable or accommodating, it's really a low confidence move people use when they're too afraid to say, *"No."*

A person with boundaries is a confident person who knows what her limits are when it comes to how other people treat her. This is your handbook for others on how you will be treated.

NEGATIVE BEHAVIOR #6: Using Name-Calling and Anger

If your relationship was full of this type of behavior before, chances are you'll try to use it now to get him back.

Since that's how you communicated previously, it's doubtful it will get him back.

This is no way to communicate, and it explains why your relationship ended. It's time to master healthier communication skills.

Many times, this type of behavior goes way down the family tree and it's *normal* in your life or the life of your ex. If this is the case, you both must make changes, or it won't work. This is one of those few situations in which you and your ex might not be able to get back together.

NEGATIVE BEHAVIOR #7: Obsessive Behavior & Misinterpreting His Behavior

Recall that your mind works overtime to trick you into believing things that aren't true.

When you find yourself obsessing over the breakup, take notes on the thoughts you keep having. What questions keep returning? Write them down.

- Will he come back?
- Does he miss me?
- Does he still love me?
- Does he love *her* more than me?
- What can I do *now* to get him back?
- Can I get him back now that he's dating someone else?
- He looks happy, does that mean he's over me?
- He's following me on Tik Tok, does that mean he wants to get back together?
- He drove by my office yesterday; is he trying to run into me?

The real answer to these questions is *nobody knows*. You cannot predict his behavior with any degree of accuracy. He may not even know the answers to some of those questions, so turning them over in your mind is just driving you crazy.

How Do You Stop?

It's easier said than done, right? You are experiencing these feelings and emotions and I'm telling you to stop as if it were that easy. Of course, if it was that easy, you wouldn't need this book, so let's look at a few strategies you can employ.

Acknowledge What You're Feeling

It's okay to feel angry, disappointed, frustrated, sad or whatever you're feeling. The trick is to acknowledge those feelings without acting out on them. That's called being reactive.

Get yourself a journal and write down these feelings. Journal about what you're feeling. Draw pictures. Write long paragraphs and cover it up with paint. Do whatever it takes to work through the feelings without allowing them to hurt your chances of getting your guy back.

Don't Wallow in These Feelings

It's easy to slip into wallowing. When you're wallowing in something, you're enjoying it. Wallowing means you like to *indulge in an unrestrained way*. You enjoy your negativity. But do you really? Is staying in this negative space that much fun?

Of course not, so recognize that you might be enjoying these negative feelings just a little too much and then decide to deal with them, instead of enjoying them.

If you're struggling to get out of your slump, get out of the house and go do something you enjoy. Take an afternoon to window shop for a new dress or shoes. Take your dog to the dog park so he can run and play. Go to the bookstore and find a book you can read and enjoy. Do something to break your rut and get you out and about.

Write a Few Sentences

This isn't really a story as much as it's a couple of sentences you can use to motivate yourself when you're struggling with negative emotions.

What can you write that will inspire you? Perhaps it's something like, *"I know that if I give myself time and I work on controlling my emotions, I will be ready for a new, healthy relationship."* You could also try something like, *"I know I'm just beginning to process this breakup and that nothing seems clear right now."*

Prioritize You

Many women prioritize the other people in their lives before they prioritize themselves. Now that you're single, spend some time on self-care. There is a chapter on self-care in Step Three to help you further, but why not get started now?

Try taking a hot bath or going for a manicure. Do something that is just for you. If you want to drag a girlfriend along for your manicure, great, just stay away from the topic of your breakup!

Avoid Places Where Your Ex Might Be

Driving by his office on the off chance that you'll get a glimpse of your ex doesn't help you squash negative emotions. Visiting the gym when you know he's usually there doesn't help you distract your mind from the breakup.

Instead, avoid some of those places he may be. If you belong to the same gym, go when you know he won't be there. If you work in the same office, try flexing your hours to see if you can reduce the chances of running into him.

Do your best to avoid encountering him, for now.

CHAPTER 7

It's Time to Set Boundaries

What are Boundaries?

A boundary is a space or a limit you place between you and someone or something else. Think of it as a fence you place to separate acceptable treatment of you from unacceptable treatment.

Use your values to create rules about how people treat you. Don't let a man convince you to have sex with him on a first date. Look at your values and establish a set of standards for how people will treat you.

Let's look at an example.

Debbie and Susan are friends, but Susan always runs behind and Debbie likes to be on time. They meet with some of their friends once a week to hang out. Susan usually picks Debbie up at her house but she's always late. Debbie has two choices. She can set a boundary with Susan, or she can continue to be late.

Debbie decides, with the help of her therapist, to set a boundary with Susan. She calls Susan to confirm their plans for the upcoming night out. Before Debbie hangs up, she tells Susan, *"I'll be ready at 8. If you're running late, I'll just go ahead by myself."*

When the night out comes, Debbie waits patiently until 8:00. At eight, Debbie gets a text from Susan, *"I'll be there in a few minutes."* Debbie texts back, *"No need. I will go on ahead without you."* Susan argues back, *"No, wait for me. I'll be there in less than ten."*

Debbie repeats her statement, *"I'll go ahead without you"* and Susan comes back once more, *"Please wait for me Debbie – less than ten I promise!"* At this point, Debbie ends the conversation by saying, *"I'll see you at the restaurant."*

Debbie set a boundary with Susan, and if you were paying attention, you noticed that Debbie also used the rule of three to hold tight to her boundary. This means she restated her boundary three times, patiently without anger or malice. What happens next?

It's possible that when Susan got to the event, she treated Debbie poorly. She may have ignored her or maybe she berated her in front of their friends. This is an attempt to make Debbie feel badly for holding to the boundary she set with Susan.

If Debbie gives Susan time, and holds to her boundaries, Susan may come around but regardless of whether Susan comes around or not, Debbie must be proud that she stuck to her boundaries and recognize that Susan is making a choice of how she reacts to them.

When you enforce boundaries, remember that your happiness matters. You are enforcing a boundary to hold tight to your own values.

When someone reacts negatively to your boundaries, that's on them. Setting boundaries helps you navigate your life and avoid being used or abused by others. Having boundaries is very important in maintaining the confidence you're rebuilding and sticking to your values.

People who do not respect your boundaries or people who punish you after you establish boundaries probably need to be let go from your life. If it's a family member, you may need to cut back the amount of time you spend with that person.

How do You Set Healthy Boundaries?

Observe and Determine Where You Need Boundaries

You might not be aware of where you need to set boundaries, so you need to be a detective in your own life. Observe how you feel in different situations:

- What makes you angry?

- When do you get frustrated?
- When do you feel hurt?
- Do you feel someone has taken advantage of you?
- Do you feel disrespected?

These are all signals your boundaries are being crossed and you need to set a boundary to alleviate those negative feelings.

Allow time

Setting boundaries is not a speedy process. You didn't get to a place where this person took advantage of you overnight. There was a pattern of behavior which led up to this point. You'll need to summon the courage and resolve to set boundaries and stick to them.

The first time Debbie told Susan she would go ahead without her, Susan became angry, but she may not have fully gotten the message. The same thing occurred the following week. It took two or three times of Debbie leaving without Susan before she really got the message and started showing up on time.

Effective Communication

One key to setting healthy boundaries is to communicate effectively. It is important to use *"I"* statements, instead of *"You"* statements. Sentences which begin with *"you"* indicate blame while sentences which begin with *"I"* tell the other person you are expressing your feelings about something. Let's look at the difference.

"You always make me late for work because you can't get out of bed on time"

Or

"I get frustrated when I am late to work all the time"

Which one would you be more responsive to? Most people would rather hear the second statement and would be more open to a discussion.

Honesty

It can feel uncomfortable to be honest with your loved ones about your feelings. You feel guilty, so you tiptoe around what you want to say instead of just coming out with it. When you can't express your true feelings about something, you're not telling someone what your boundaries are.

I know it will be difficult to speak honestly about your feelings if you're not accustomed to doing so, but it's something you need to do if you want to move forward and be a more confident woman.

Allow For Consequences

There are two types of consequences, natural and logical. Natural consequences happen without your intervention. For example, if a child pokes around in the morning and doesn't get ready when he's told to, he'll be late for school. You could bail him out and take him so he's on time but then he won't learn anything about his behavior. Allowing him to arrive late is a natural consequence.

In relationships, people insulate loved ones from consequences, even if it's at their own expense. Your ex may have had a drug or drinking problem that you made excuses for, or even covered with your own actions.

To have consequences, you need to issue a warning like this, *"If you don't get ready for school, you're going to be late."* Next, hold tight to your warning and don't bail your child out.

This isn't the same as threatening someone. If a child doesn't do their homework, they will get a failing grade for it. That's a natural consequence. If your boyfriend drinks all the time, you stop calling his work to make excuses for him, *"Jim is home sick today."* You let him get fired. Allowing natural consequences to occur is not fun, but you need to do it regardless.

The example of Debbie and Susan above is an example of logical consequences. You tell someone, if *A* happens, you will do *B*. You must be able to follow through as Debbie did. Remember in the example, Debbie didn't say *"You're always late. If you're late tonight I will go without you."* Instead, Debbie said, *"I'll be ready at eight. If you're not here, I will go ahead by myself."* It would have been okay even for Debbie to have said, *"I don't like being late to meet with our friends all the time."*

When you are talking about consequences, you are giving the other person a choice. If you do *X, Y* will happen. This is true of either natural or logical consequences.

Be Brief

You don't need to provide a big, detailed explanation for your boundary. When you lay out the consequence, be succinct. *"If you're not here by eight, I will just go ahead without you."* It's not long and drawn out.

When you set a boundary, the person you're setting it with will ask for an explanation. You do **not** need to clarify your position. You also don't lie. Let's look at another example.

Emily and Jen have been friends for several years but during that time, Jen has pushed Emily around, invalidated her feelings and treated her disrespectfully. After seeking therapy for her low self-esteem, Emily decided it was time to put an end to being treated poorly.

Jen was having a party, something she did often, and Emily usually went but this time, she decided she would not go. Her urge was to lie to Jen and tell her she had somewhere else to go but her therapist encouraged her to be brief.

Emily simply told Jen that she was not coming, resisting the urge to provide an explanation. Her therapist had warned her that Jen would ask for, even demand an explanation. Emily simply said, *"I'm sorry Jen, I cannot attend."* She left it at that. It was difficult for her, but she did it.

You must do the same. A boundary crasher wants you to give an explanation so they can argue with it or debunk it. You don't owe anyone an explanation for holding to your boundaries.

This is Going to Suck at First

Setting boundaries is not fun. It's going to make you feel uneasy and uncomfortable. The only way through this feeling is straight through. Power through, feel uncomfortable and know that each time you do it, it will get a little easier and you will feel a little bit of self-esteem return. You will feel more confident each time you stand up for yourself.

Choose Your Battles

When you're setting boundaries, don't tackle everything at once. After you've completed your observations and you know where boundaries need to be set, look the list over and pick two or three to work on first.

Which boundaries are bothering you the most? Those are the ones you want to tackle first. Understand why you are choosing to set that boundary, so you are clear and firm in setting it and standing up for yourself.

Mean What You Say

If you set a boundary and then give in to someone who tries to crash it, your credibility is as good as gone. When you set a boundary, be prepared to stand behind what you say.

When Debbie told Susan she was going to leave at eight if she wasn't there, the best thing she did was to follow through and *really* leave at eight, as promised. If she had waited until Susan got there, she wouldn't have been able to get Susan to show up on time or believe her ultimatum again. If you say you're going to do something or not do something, that's what you must stand by.

This Isn't About Their Feelings, It's About Yours

People pleasers do so because they don't want to hurt someone's feelings. They say yes to keep the peace. When you begin to set boundaries, you may feel as if you're going to hurt the boundary crashers feelings.

Setting boundaries is about staying true to your values. It is not about someone else's feelings. You may not like knowing someone is angry with you, but you must learn how to sit with these feelings and get comfortable in them.

The more you practice, it will get easier, and you will come to realize one important fact. The boundary crasher did not care about your feelings when they pushed you beyond acceptable limits and now, you need to take care of yourself. You cannot hold true to your own values and worry about someone else's feelings at the same time. What you should be asking yourself is why this person doesn't care about your feelings.

If that doesn't work for you, think of it this way – saying yes to one thing means you're saying no to something else. Saying yes to allowing someone to crash your boundaries means saying no to your own values.

Prepare

Before you set a boundary with someone, it's helpful to prepare. This may sound silly, but it works. Let's imagine that your sister always insists you shop together for your mother's Christmas gift, but she always forces her own choice on you and it's usually a gift you know your mother either doesn't need or won't like.

This year, you decide you're not going to go shopping with your sister. You're going to get your own gift. To prepare for setting this boundary, practice.

Prepare your own words first. When she calls to set up your annual shopping trip, what will you say? Play the conversation in your head, or even better, write it out and say it out loud. Like everything else, the more senses you use the more real it will become.

> Your sister: *"Hey! When do you want to go shopping for Mom's birthday? I can do either Saturday or Sunday. What works for you?"*
>
> You: *"Actually, I am just going to get Mom a gift myself this year."*
>
> Your sister: *"What? Seriously? But we always go in together to get Mom something. Come on – go with me. Don't break tradition!"*

You might be tempted now, so really practice this part.

> You: *"No, I'm just going to get Mom a gift myself."*
>
> Your sister: *"I can't believe you're doing this to me! You know how much fun we always have shopping together! What is your problem?!?!?!"*
>
> You: *"I really need to run. I'll see you at the party!"*

Get a friend to play your sister and prompt her about what to say. If you find someone who knows your sister, even better because she can play the role without prompting. Any preparation you do before speaking with your sister will help you get through it.

Remember, you have three goals – to hold true to your own values, to avoid answering any questions and to stick to your guns. Do not give in.

Why Do Boundaries Matter?

You want your ex back, right? Often, men are the ones who trounce boundaries. Did you ex disrespect you? Did he overrule the boundaries you set, or did you let him run all over you because you never set boundaries?

This is important because men are attracted to women who stand by their boundaries. Maybe he left because he lost respect for you because you had few boundaries.

This will change for him to see…for all to see!

CHAPTER 8

Don't Freak Out When He Starts Dating

The worst thing imaginable has happened: your ex is dating someone else. You. Are. Freaking. Out. Okay, take a deep breath, because him dating someone else doesn't mean what you think it does. Not even close.

Why is He Dating Someone Else?

First, let's lay to rest any rumors about why he's dating someone else. In your mind, you're imagining all kinds of scenarios. She's prettier than you, she's got better boobs than you, she's smarter, sexier, or whatever else you conjure up.

No. No. And no. She most likely is the first living, breathing female who has shown interest in him since the breakup, and because he feels crappy right now, he has started dating her.

Why?

Because if he's dating someone else, he doesn't have to face the misery of the breakup. Yes, even if he broke up with you, that doesn't mean he's happy right now. The fact that he jumped into a new relationship probably says he's not happy.

If He's Miserable, Why Does He Look Happy?

You can blame society for this one. When you break up with someone, everyone expects you to move on as if nothing happened. Get back on the horse. He was a dud anyway; why are you crying over that jerk, and so on. They think they're helping, but of course, they aren't.

Men are usually conditioned not to show negative emotions, leaving them with happy emotions, real or not. He can't show any signs of weakness. It isn't manly.

If you see him on social media looking happy with his new girl, it's time to block them both. These images won't help you move forward, even though you know it's not him in love, but rather him in denial.

What You're Thinking and How to Counter Those Thoughts

Are His Friends and Family Comparing Her to Me?

The answer is probably not. His family may not ever meet her, especially if they really liked you. He doesn't want to hear the comparisons. He's already making them himself.

As for the rest, who knows, and really, who cares? You can decide whatever you want here, so go for broke. Decide they don't like her and move on. It has no impact on your life. She's the rebound.

Why do I Hate/Love Her?

One of two things will happen when you think about the new girl. Either you'll instantly hate her because she has what you want, or you'll secretly love her because she's everything you wish you were.

Rather than fixate on liking or hating her, consider that soon she'll be in your shoes. Regard her as being in your breakup sisterhood. She is worthy of your respect until she proves otherwise.

How Can I Avoid Getting Angry All Over Again?

I know, you feel in control again and now anger is rearing its ugly head. Anger is a valid emotion, but what's the point really? Anger may be valid, but it's unproductive. Instead, remember that a breakup means something was broken.

If you want to get him back, anger is not your path forward. Fixing what's broken inside you and moving toward being a happy, independent woman is a path forward. Take a few breaths and remember, she is the rebound.

How Can I Stop Fixating on Them?

So, all of this hasn't worked, and you're still fixated on them. Grab a friend who will listen, and that might be challenging if you've worn them all out talking about this already, and ask that friend if she'll hear you out, just one more time.

Talk through it and ask her to listen, then when you're done, let it go. Fixating on it is not going to move you forward. Remember that getting him back involves you doing things he doesn't expect. He expects you to fixate on this, so don't. Let it go.

How Can I Avoid Becoming Promiscuous?

An obvious solution to getting over him dating someone else is to date someone else yourself. The problem is that if you found someone new to date, and you'd likely do what he did, which is to date the first person who shows an interest, you will be resigned to the same fate as him. I've just spent a few hundred words telling you why this won't work for him, and that is to say that it won't work for you either.

You're delaying dealing with the real issues. I'm all for you dating other guys, but not just yet. You aren't quite ready. Don't worry, I'll let you know when you are. Deal?

Meanwhile, understand that you should start looking within to find the acceptance you want to seek from outside influences. Your worth is not determined by which guy you date or how quickly you get back to dating. Your worth is something you determine from within, and you'll work on it soon!

Why Is My Playlist All Sad Songs?

This is natural. You want someone to commiserate with you and who better than a crooner singing about his lost love? Listening to sad songs is all well and good, but if you have a sad song playlist, then you also need a suck it up and deal playlist. Get yourself some upbeat songs that make you want to shake your booty while you're scrubbing toilets and play it after the sad songs have run out.

Your Healthy Course Forward

Practice Self-Awareness

When you are self-aware, you are aware of what you're thinking about. You are internally experiencing your world.

It's easy to allow your mind to wander to the negative thoughts around your ex and his new girlfriend. When you do this, remember that you're thinking about something that probably isn't happening right now and may not even be true.

Become Mindful

When you are mindful, you are tuned into your thoughts. Sometimes those thoughts wander into unproductive territory.

You're either working with anxiety over the future or ruminating over events of the past. Neither of those will move you forward.

That leaves you with staying present in the moment. Stop and use your senses for a few moments.

What do you see? Are there beautiful flowers out your window? Is the sky a particularly pretty shade of blue?

What do you hear? Birds chirping? The whine of your computer? The sound of cars or rain pounding on the street outside?

What do you smell? Did someone in the office just make popcorn? Do you have some sweet-smelling flowers on your desk?

What do you taste? Enjoy a snack and savor the flavors. Focus just on the taste and nothing else.

What do you feel, with your fingers? The smoothness of your desk? The softness of an afghan lying over the sofa?

All these activities help you focus your energy on right now and away from anxiety and rumination.

Shift Your Thoughts to Something Positive

You're aware of your thoughts and mindfully present in this moment. The last piece is to shift your thoughts to something positive and fun. Imagine the girl's night you have planned with your friends this week or the new car you will be picking up tomorrow.

It sounds cliché but think happy thoughts.

Lather, Rinse and Repeat

You may go through these three steps multiple times a day at first and that's okay. It's normal, but as you become more self-aware and practice mindfulness more often, you'll experience more happy thoughts and fewer thoughts of your ex.

Your best defense to dealing with him dating someone new is a good offense, which means presenting the best possible version of yourself, especially if there's a chance it will get back to him. And yes, even if you block him on social media, he *will* find out.

CHAPTER 9

The Best Ways to Alleviate Your Anxiety

Anxiety is a feeling of intense worry that comes along when you're facing something stressful, often a situation where you don't know what the outcome might be.

Sometimes, anxiety can make you more productive. It can push you toward meeting a deadline or keep you safe in a scary situation.

Other times, anxiety can be debilitating and derail your best laid plans to move forward productively.

These are anxious thoughts:

- If I get an F on this exam, my whole future is ruined, and I'll never get a good job anywhere
- If I can't get my ex back, I'll never be able to find another guy who will date me

- I need to lose ten pounds, or my ex will never take another look at me and then I'll be alone forever
- If I can't prove to my boss that I can handle this project, I'll lose my job, and then I won't be able to afford my apartment and my car will be repossessed

These thoughts are *what if* scenarios your mind conjures up to travel down a worst-case scenario pathway.

If you have anxious moments, know that you aren't alone. It's one of the most diagnosed mental health problems. I know this doesn't help you feel better, so let's find something that might.

What Factors Play a Role in Experiencing Anxiety?

Genetics

Look at your family tree. The chances are that there's anxiety somewhere. Genetics play a large role in many mental health issues. This doesn't mean you *will* have anxiety if others in your family have experienced it, but it does improve your odds.

Other Mental Health Issues

Sometimes, anxiety piggybacks along with other mental health disorders, like depression or some eating disorders. Those disorders cause some cognitive and emotional distortions that increase your anxiety and present a challenge when it comes to dealing with anxiety.

Gender

Statistics tell us that women are more likely than men to experience certain types of anxiety disorders, of which there are several.

Your Culture and Family Background

Sometimes we're raised in an environment that manages anxiety and stress differently. Some cultures deal with anxiety differently, leaving us unable to cope. These cultural differences determine whether you'll be able to recognize anxiety for what it is and how you deal with it. Sometimes, it isn't even cultural but familial. If your parents don't believe in things like anxiety, you might have been raised to ignore it.

Your Own World

External forces like work, school, family, and other relationships can lead to anxiety. Your job could be extra stressful during a busy season, like holidays or Black Friday if you work retail. Your company might be up for a big project, and everyone is on edge. If you're in school, tedious homework assignments and big projects, as well as exams can add stress and anxiety.

And family, well, family always carries the potential to add stress and anxiety, whether they do it on purpose or not. Illness, death and even happy events like new babies, engagements and weddings can all play a part.

The Circumstances of Your Breakup

Your ex may be adding to your anxiety. Not just because he broke up with you, but in the way he did it. He may have laid all the blame on you or lied to you about why he wanted to break up, leaving you feeling confused and anxious.

Either shouldering the blame or being confused about why he really left can be confusing. Remember, your mind is addicted to those love hormones and it's playing tricks on you.

The Stage of Grief You're Experiencing

Some of the stages of grieving a relationship will cause more anxiety than others. For example, if you're experiencing the denial phase, your mind is denying that the breakup even happened and is working out possible scenarios to make things right again.

External and internal bargaining can also make you feel anxious as you begin searching for solutions – pathways to a repaired relationship. The *"If I do this, that will happen"* type of scenarios are anxiety in high gear.

Other stages can present anxious moments too, so being aware of those stages and how they're impacting your mind and body will help you alleviate the anxiety being created.

How to Manage Anxiety

There are many things you can do to manage your anxiety. Let's look at a few now.

Implement a Self-Care Routine

One of the best ways to work on anxious feelings is with a self-care routine. Some women shift their focus from themselves to their guy. As natural nurturers, it's easy to allow this to happen without recognizing it.

Self-care means taking time out just for you, spending time doing something you enjoy, something that calms you and brings you peace. It isn't just about taking a bubble bath. It's about learning to value you and dedicate time to taking care of you.

There are several things you can do to practice self-care, especially during this time:

- Take a warm bath – try some essential oils, candles, or meditative music
- Meditate - calm your mind
- Take a nap – anxiety can cause sleepless nights
- Journal – get those anxious thoughts down on paper
- Hang out with friends – just to have fun! You remember fun, right?
- Take a day off – take a mental health day and do something fun
- Listen to music – but make it uplifting music, not breakup songs
- Do something outdoors – take a hike, clean out flower beds, take a walk downtown
- Do something creative – anything that shifts the focus of your mind will help
- Exercise – this is an excellent way to counteract the chemicals associated with anxiety

- Eat comfort food – don't binge eat, but if a dish of macaroni and cheese makes you feel good, go for it
- Organize something – this is a great way to shift your focus and get your mind off your worries
- Seek therapy – sometimes, anxiety is just too difficult to overcome, or it is associated with depression; there's no shame in therapy!

Practice Mindfulness

Mindfulness is about living in the here and now; it's about becoming aware of your thoughts and surroundings.

Part of using mindfulness is acknowledging anxious feelings and labeling them. You naturally want to avoid pain, which will cause your overall mental health to decline.

When you practice mindfulness, you say to yourself, *"Right now, I feel angry with Doug for leaving me with two kids, a dog and a mortgage while he goes off and finds himself a teenager."* Or *"I feel so lonely right now without Joe here to watch a movie with. I don't even want to turn on Netflix because it reminds me of him."*

It's okay to acknowledge those feelings, as long as your next move is to allow them to keep flowing through you and avoid allowing them to sit and fester like an open wound. Just remember the leaf floating down the stream.

Be Grateful

Right now, much of your focus is on what you've lost. Get a journal and write down things for which you're grateful, like this: *"I am grateful for the barista at Starbucks who knows my order and has it ready by the time I get to the front of the line."* Or *"I am grateful for the fond memories of the trip Josh and I took to the apple orchard last fall."*

It's okay to be grateful for something good that you had in your relationship. In fact, soon, you'll use those fond memories to play with his psyche!

Practicing gratitude enables you to focus on the good things in your life, instead of the negatives. It helps you be more mindful and present in the current moment.

Do Something You Love

If you've read any of my books, you know I'm a huge proponent of having hobbies and things about which you have a lot of passion. For example, I'm passionate about animals, cats in particular.

Hobbies help you keep busy and busy is a great way to be! Hobbies also provide you with the opportunity to build your confidence and excel at something.

When you have a hobby, you not only become good at something, which builds your confidence, but you get out and meet new people who share your interest. You build friendships and might even find a great guy along the way, if you're in the market for one, of course.

When you are busy, you aren't free 24/7 for that beck-and-call date. This puts a guy in chase mode if he's truly interested in you. If he isn't, his loss. But a guy who sees it as a challenge to get time on your calendar will work for what he wants. He will chase you, which is what he likes best!

Spend Time with Friends and Family

If you have family out of town, that can be the best thing for a little distraction! Get yourself away from all the reminders of your relationship. Of course, you can't run away forever, but the goal is to create a mental distraction and move your thoughts away from those anxious thoughts regarding your ex.

it is best to avoid talking about your ex and the breakup while you are away, unless you think you can discuss them without feeling anxious. Don't stuff down your feelings, but if you can keep yourself and your family from spending hours bad-mouthing your ex, you'll enjoy your visit more.

Let Go of Needing to Know Why

A lot of your anxiety is probably focused on why he left and what you did wrong. If you don't agree, refer again to the stages of grieving a relationship. If you haven't gone through this yet, you will.

There is no such thing as closure. It's a word some folks use to try to say they've settled the negative thing that happened, but the truth is that closure is elusive. Knowing the why won't make you feel better, and it certainly won't change the outcome.

CHAPTER 10

How Do I Know When I'm Ready to Move to Step 2?

You are ready to move to Step Two when you aren't spending every day with a Kleenex in your hand and red swollen eyes or pounding your fist in anger. That's the highly emotional state you're trying to alleviate.

It's okay to still be angry, but don't allow it to rule every waking moment. Feeling the anger and allowing it to move on through means you're healthier and ready to move forward.

You're ready for step two when you've experienced the stage of grieving called Initial Acceptance, which will morph into acceptance and hope. You will cycle through these stages multiple times and each time, the positive feelings increasingly outweigh the negative feelings. It isn't enough to go through acceptance once. You'll go through it two or three times before you feel better.

Another signal is when you've stopped the negative behaviors that are ruining your chances of getting him back. A healthy mind has moved past these and is ready to press on in a positive way.

You aren't feeling as much anxiety as you were. Everyone experiences anxiety, but it isn't consuming your life. If it is, seeking a professional therapist is your next step.

When your mind is overly emotional, it's impossible to think rationally. Find a healthy balance between your emotional mind and your rational mind, so you're operating with your wise mind.

Thinking back, you probably can recognize when you felt incapable of making good decisions. You had trouble functioning at work if you needed to use rational thought processes.

Now, you feel as if you can fully function and be present in the moment. Of course, there will still be moments when you slip backwards and that's okay.

The next step is all about assessing the breakup. This will cause you to make that slip, but you're healthier now and you have many tools at your disposal to help you pull yourself out of the doldrums that may arise.

So, to reiterate, here's your checklist:

- I no longer feel like I'm in a very emotional state all the time
- I have experienced the acceptance stage of grieving my relationship three times, each time feeling better than the time before
- I have stopped the negative behaviors in Chapter Six
- I don't have as many anxious moments and when I do, I can use the tools provided to move past my anxiety
- I have sought out professional help if I felt it was necessary
- I am thinking with my wise mind, at least most of the time

step 2

Assessing the Breakup

Now, you're at Step Two and I have just one question to ask you before we move forward. Have you overcome the anxiety and emotions of the breakup? Are you now thinking with your wise mind?

If you are, great! Let's continue, but if you still feel emotional, you aren't ready for this step just yet, and that's okay. Remember, you're not in a hurry here. You want to move through these steps effectively, not quickly. It's kind of like baking bread – if you don't wait for the yeast to rise, the bread won't be any good. If you don't take the time to overcome your emotions, your attempts during this step will be disappointing for you.

Step Two is where you assess what happened in the breakup. You need to be brutally honest with yourself about what really happened. The rose-colored glasses must come off so the reality of the situation can come forward.

This relationship is in the past. If the two of you get back together, it's a new relationship and the old one is history. To move forward successfully together, something must change.

Imagine trying to learn something new, like baking cookies. You've never baked a cookie before in your life, but you're going to try. Rather than reading a recipe, you get out eggs, sugar, salt, butter and maybe something extra like chocolate chips. You mix everything up and put it on a cookie sheet. You pop it in the oven but as soon as it heats up, the dough just flattens and spreads all over the pan.

You toss that batch and repeat the steps exactly as you did before, not changing anything in the recipe. Of course, you will have the same result.

It's the same with relationships. Something must change for the two of you to experience a successful second attempt at a relationship. You cannot control him, but you can control you.

However, if you don't stop and examine what went wrong, you don't know what to fix or modify.

This step will help you understand:

- How he's feeling about the breakup – what's going on in his head
- That he most likely lied to you about the reason for your breakup and why that's impeding your progress
- The number one reason many couples break up
- Why it's time to take him down from his pedestal and how to make it happen
- What he's thinking right now about your relationship and why he needs time apart from you
- The importance of being honest with yourself about how you feel about the breakup
- Whether you miss him or just having someone in your life
- If he's healthy enough and capable of love
- Why missing him isn't the same as loving him
- What your role was in the breakup and how you can do damage control

CHAPTER 11

What He's Thinking & Doing Right Now

While it may seem as if your ex has things all neatly wrapped up because he initiated the breakup, that is far from the truth. He's a mess too, regardless of his outward appearance. He doesn't know whether he's coming or going most of the time.

Most people think men aren't as deeply affected by a breakup as women are, but this isn't true. They are affected, they just don't show it.

What Is He Thinking?

He has moments when he questions the breakup and he's asking himself as many questions as you are about what happened. He is, however, asking different questions. His questions and train of thought go more like this:

- Why did I break up with her?

- Why did she do that to me?
- Why did I do that to her?
- Why can't I find someone to love?
- Why can't I love?
- Boy it's great to be single again!
- Is she going to date that guy from the gym now that I'm out of the picture?
- What is she thinking/feeling right now?
- Do I need a dog?

His confusion and these emotions, and not the reasons he gave you, are the reasons for the breakup. He got confused and when a man is facing emotional turmoil or confusion, he backs away so he can lick his wounds and reassess what's going on.

Reading that might make you to think he needs you to nurture and help him. Perhaps it made you feel sorry for him. **Don't**. He doesn't need nurturing right now; he needs time with his own thoughts and emotions.

A man can and will fix his own problems if he has some confidence and self-esteem. If he doesn't, he may stay stuck in this rut. **This is not your fault, and this is not your problem to solve**.

While it's true that men show their love for women by doing things to help them, it's not often how they receive love. For his own sense of male pride, he must fix his own problems, mostly by himself. If he needs help from you or anyone else, a strong, confident man will ask for it.

Your ex may seem happy in that new rebound relationship, but oftentimes men have difficulty forming a real romantic relationship after a breakup. He too may get stuck in the past and this will limit his ability to make a long-term commitment.

In fact, there are a whole range of ways that breakups can affect men that might not even cross your mind, for example, staying stuck in the past can make him temporarily impotent. While this is an extreme reaction to a breakup, it can happen and it's something he may need to seek therapy for.

If you run into your ex following your breakup, he might pretend not to care. This is simply his way of deflecting his true emotions. He can't deal with them, so he puts on a mask of indifference. While it can feel hurtful, you must understand the underlying cause – he's in pain and he isn't ready to deal with it.

What Is He Doing?

Chances are your ex will have a rebound relationship. You already read about rebound relationships, so you know not to worry about this. In fact, he may not just have one rebound relationship, he may have several. Even though there may be more than one, the reason is the same. What are these relationships doing for him?

- Helping him avoid coping with his feelings over the breakup
- Surrounding him with women who show an interest in him – he's not alone
- Enabling him to avoid the less-than-comfortable feeling he has about the breakup
- Boosting his self-esteem
- Making him feel as if he's still desirable
- Proving something to him, and you, namely that he's still got it
- Helping him catch up on missed opportunities

He may engage in addictive behaviors, especially if he has an addictive personality. If he's battled drugs or alcohol before, he may dive in again. This self-destruction is a way for him to get back at you if he feels you somehow ruined his life. It's all about him and you have no role or blame in his actions.

Some men seek revenge after a breakup. If he feels you were the cause of him leaving, he may strike out at you and try to hurt you back. Guys do this by sharing previously secret information, images of you that you may not want others to see or videos. Usually, these behaviors come from a guy that you broke up with, but if he somehow blames you for everything that went wrong, he may try it.

When he isn't seeking rebound relationships, your ex is spending time by himself, regardless of what he wants you to believe.

He needs this alone time to process the relationship and what happened. Men can't deal with heavy emotions when they're in a group. He needs to do that alone.

During his alone time, he's running through all his reasons for breaking up with you and searching for validation. He will come up with everything you did to cause him to take that action. Recall what you learned about him having negative feelings about the breakup. This is where they're coming from and why he needs time away from you.

He will seek out his friends. He may feel he's been forced to spend less time with them than he preferred during your relationship and now, he wants to rekindle those friendships. He also wants to be around his friends because he trusts them, and he needs someone he can trust around him right now.

Now that he has more time to himself, a guy might pick up a new hobby or start playing a sport. He can improve himself and have some fun doing it. This also sends a signal to him that he doesn't *need* to be in a relationship to have fun. This is all good stuff.

He may also try to call you, but this might not be for a few weeks yet. He's felt hurt, just like you, and now, he's craving that intimacy you shared. He's starting to miss you when this happens. BAM!

An opposite reaction to most of the above is that a guy may do nothing, and by nothing, I mean *nothing*. He may move through life as if he's a robot, doing the daily routine but nothing more. It doesn't mean he's depressed; it just means he's doing nothing. It's his way of figuring out how he feels and dealing with it.

Some men will dig into work responsibilities after a breakup. This is an escape mechanism, designed to distract him from his thoughts and feelings over the breakup. He is experiencing emotions he doesn't quite know what to do with and the obvious way to avoid that is to bury himself in work.

When a guy talks to his friends about the breakup, he will distort the truth of the breakup. It'll go something like this:

- She was too clingy and needy
- We decided to breakup together – it was mutual
- I never really liked her that much anyway
- I was gonna break up with her eventually anyway, why not now?

He knows these statements aren't true, but they help him validate his actions.

He will blame you. Very infrequently, a man will take all the blame upon himself. More often, he will blame you for *everything*. All this is doing is giving him a false sense of control over the situation. Unfortunately for him, without accepting any responsibility for what happened, he's setting up his future relationships for failure, including any reconciliation with you.

Your ex may institute his own no contact rule. Most, but not all men will destroy all memories of you shortly after your breakup. Don't be surprised when you discover that the notes and mementos you gave him are gone. That's okay. It's time to build new memories anyway!

He will block you on social media and delete photos of you on his phone. He will avoid places he knows you frequent. This is all to avoid the memories of your relationship. It helps him heal faster and deal with his negative emotions.

Eventually, your ex will begin to miss you. While he thought he would be happier without you, he's discovered that the grass isn't as green on this side of your relationship as he had hoped. Maybe women aren't fawning all over him, as he imagined they would be. Perhaps his friends have told him he made a huge mistake. He's dealt with the negativity and he's now questioning his decision.

This is what you want him to be doing.

Understanding what your ex is thinking and feeling should help you navigate the remainder of the steps. By now, you're past the highly emotional state and this relationship assessment will help you determine what you can do to move forward and get him back.

CHAPTER 12

He Lied to You

Why do men lie about breakups? One reason is because he doesn't want to hurt your feelings, as strange as that sounds. He may also want you to maintain your idealized image of him, meaning that he will lie in order to protect that image.

Finally, he may do it out of self-preservation. He knows the truth, but if he lies about it, he doesn't need to face it.

THE FIRST LIE: It's Not You, It's Me

This is code for *I'm about to break your heart, but I want to look good while doing it.* This reason probably is about him, but he's not willing to admit it to you or anyone else. Unfortunately, if your guy gave you this reason, there might not be a reconciliation in your future.

THE SECOND LIE: I Need Some Time on My Own aka I Need Space

This reason is really saying he isn't interested in you and wants to put distance between you. The reasons for him wanting this distance are many. They range from him dealing with something difficult, such as the death of a loved one, on down to basic selfishness on his part.

In some instances, if a guy requests space to work through something difficult, he might come back, but if he truly isn't interested in you and your relationship is somewhat young, he may not.

THE THIRD LIE: We Need a Break

Raise your hand if your mind instantly went to the series, *Friends*. When a guy says this, what he's really saying is we need a break**up**. While he's indicating there is hope for a reconciliation, this might be his way of stringing you along.

There is hope if your guy used this line on you. Maybe he did just need a break to deal with stuff. It's too soon to tell.

THE FOURTH LIE: Things Have Changed, You're Not the Same Person

Of course, you aren't the same person. Neither is he, but he's using this as an excuse to end things with you. We all grow and change throughout our lives, and it's true that couples do grow apart, especially if one grows more than the other.

It's possible that one of you has grown more confident and now the balance is off. This is okay, you aren't the same woman now as you were when he broke up with you either. We'll soon see how he likes *that*.

THE FIFTH LIE: I Need to Focus on Myself for a While

This might not be a lie but the reasons behind it aren't altruistic. Many men go through this self-important stage of life. They decide that being the best at their career is like giving themselves as a giant gift to mankind. He might conclude that it's his obligation to the human race to thrive and be strong. His final decision is that a relationship with anyone will get in the way of his drive to save humanity.

When a man is with a woman who is good for him, he will accomplish all this. A man who's truly in love will work hard to make both things click in his life. He will strive to spend time with you, and he will work harder at his job. He will seek a balance, not tip the scales against you.

THE SIXTH LIE: You Deserve Someone Who Loves You for You

Unfortunately for you, this is him telling you he doesn't love you and your chances of reconciliation aren't very good.

Having said that, something about you attracted him to you, so there is a chance that when he sees the new and improved you from Step Three, he will change his mind, but it's important not to pin all your hopes on that chance.

THE SEVENTH LIE: The Timing Isn't Right

He may say this because he's dealing with something heavy, and he can't handle the emotions of that *and* his emotions for you.

There's no such thing as good timing. When a relationship clicks and it's right, timing doesn't matter. If he needs time to deal with something bad, like losing his job or putting the final touches on his divorce, give him that time and space and he may return.

THE EIGHTH LIE: You Need to Get Out There and Explore Life

Uh huh. Who is *this* guy to tell you what you need? This is his way of saying he doesn't want to date you any longer, but instead of being up front with you, he's blaming it on you. Nobody but you should decide whether your life experiences are where they should be.

And anyway, why not explore together? This guy might be a lost cause as far as reconciliation goes.

THE NINTH LIE: You're too Good for Me

HA! This is probably true if he's using this as his excuse. Most likely, he wants to cheat on you, and he knows you won't put up with his shenanigans.

If he truly feels he isn't on your level and he's interested in you, he will figure out how to get on your level. He will work hard at becoming worthy of you. Otherwise, you just broke up with someone who's still immature and your best response may be later pal.

Drum Roll Please . . .
THE TENTH LIE: I'm Not Good Enough for You

While this one sounds like the last, the meaning behind is slightly different. In this case, he has probably already cheated on you, and he feels like a worthless ass for doing so. This is his cowardly way of telling you he's looking for or has already found someone else.

CHAPTER 13

The #1 Cause of Relationship Failure - Communication

How Communication Causes Breakups

Good, no, *great* communication should be the foundation of *every* relationship you have; no matter if it's a boyfriend, husband, boss, employee, friend, or family member. Yet, communication is a skill many people lack.

Most people don't realize that communication is a two-way street, but it's a different street than they think. The street you think you're on is one where two people are talking and everyone is listening, but really, the street you're on is one where nobody is listening. If you aren't talking, you're conjuring your reply, which will one-up whatever you're partially hearing.

Communication isn't two people talking at one another. It's one person speaking while the other listens. It's the listening part we have trouble with.

Why Does Communication Break Down?

Everyone Has Their Own Agenda

- When you have a conversation with someone, there is an agenda. It might be any one of the following, or something else
- You want to learn more about them
- You want to gain something from them
- You want to prove to yourself that you're somehow better than they are
- You have a dispute with them and want to let them know (notice I didn't say solve the dispute)

There are surely other reasons for communicating with someone, but those are the reasons you'll learn about right now.

We Don't Know How to Listen

Most people come into a conversation with their agenda in hand and they have little to no interest in hearing what the other person has to say. Even if your agenda is to learn something about the other person, while they're speaking, you're probably formulating your own story so that it sounds as good as, if not better than theirs.

The minute another person starts talking, your mind races to formulate your reply. That isn't listening. That's trying to one-up someone.

Listening involves shaking off the urge to formulate your reply until the other person has finished their statement. *Then and only then* do you begin to decide what you will say.

You Aren't Paying Attention

How many times have you been in the middle of a conversation, only to realize the other person has drifted away and is thinking about something else? You can see it by the far-away look in their eyes. Of course, the reverse of this is when you're the one who drifts off and you're left with the awkward moment of saying, *"I'm sorry, my mind wandered away for a second. Could you repeat the question?"*

This is rude behavior and tells the other person that whatever they have to say is unimportant to you, therefore you're tolerating them but not listening.

You're Emotionally Not in a Place to Listen

Sometimes, you're in an emotional moment and whatever someone else is saying to you just falls on deaf ears. You're so caught up in your own emotions that listening to someone else feels like a huge burden, too heavy to bear.

Hopefully, the person with whom you're speaking recognizes that you're not in a place to have their discussion at this time, but if they don't, it's okay to ask them to delay the conversation for a little while until you can get things under control.

You Don't Understand One Another's Communication Styles

There are three different communication styles. Most people tend to be a blend of all three, but some folks clearly lean toward one style.

See if you can identify your style.

People who practice the **aggressive** communication style are difficult to talk to. They come off as bullies because it's their way or the highway. They're always right and there's no telling them otherwise. Their favorite conversational weapons are sarcasm, condescension, and patronizing.

This type of conversationalist rarely acknowledges the good work of others and tends to stand in a rigid posture, to emulate their rigid stance on everything. This is a low-confidence person who can't admit when he's wrong. There is no point in arguing with a person practicing the aggressive style of communication. You can't win, regardless of how hard you try. Your best bet is to let them rant and then move on.

People who practice the **passive** communication style are dream partners for the aggressive conversationalist because they never raise their voice and often choose not to be heard. The passive conversationalist doesn't want to make waves and generally believes everyone in the world has more rights than they do.

This type of person rarely speaks up for herself or stands up to say what she believes in. When there is conflict between two other people, a passive conversationalist will choose both sides, so as not to anger anyone. This is also a low-confidence person who is afraid that if he speaks his opinions, others won't like him, so he keeps them to himself.

You should encourage this type of conversationalist to add their input. Ask for and show genuine interest in their point of view. If you ask for their opinion, understand that it's very difficult for them to deliver it and they're very worried about how you will respond. Therefore, it's important to show the person that their input has value by paying close attention and acknowledging their input.

The last type of communication style is **assertive**. This type of person is a great listener who believes that others can have an input into whatever he's doing. He sees the value in other people and what they can contribute. He seeks out the ideas and opinions of others and genuinely wants to help when needed. He uses an open body language and doesn't attempt to intimidate through his body. This is a confident communication style, and it should be your goal.

This person is easy to talk to but that doesn't mean he's a pushover. Apply your best listening skills and prepare to be asked for your input. This person will be a wonderful person to talk with.

How These Play a Role in Breakups

Listening is key in successful communication. You need to truly *hear* what the other person is saying so you can begin to understand their position.

Not feeling heard is a common complaint among couples who've split up. *He never listens to me.* It's very frustrating to have something important to say and feel as if you're speaking into a void where everything you say just falls off and dies somewhere.

What Is Active Listening?

Now that you understand how important communication is, and what a large role listening plays, it's time to learn about active listening.

Knowing the communication style of your conversational partner is the first step in active listening, because it will determine how you respond to that person.

How do you practice active listening? Let's find out!

Step 1: Clear Your Head

Before entering a conversation with someone, take a few moments to clear your mind. Stop and take a few deep breaths. Try to dismiss any thoughts that may be lingering and prepare yourself to just listen.

Remember, your challenge is to set aside your own agenda, at least temporarily, and truly hear what the other person has to say.

Step 2: Create Open Body Language

Don't stand with your arms folded across your chest as this is very closed body language. Use an open body stance with your arms at your sides. Lean into the speaker slightly, indicating that you're paying attention.

Turn your body so you are squared to face them. We always face the most important thing in the room with our bodies. Look at the speaker while she's talking and smile. Use appropriate facial expressions as they're required. Obviously if the person is telling you their grandmother died, a smile might not be the most appropriate facial expression.

Step 3: Encourage the Speaker

While it's rude to interrupt, it isn't rude to encourage the speaker to continue. Interrupting is more about stopping their conversational flow to inject your own *better* story. Helping the conversation along is more about asking appropriate questions at opportune moments. Make sure to wait two to three seconds to ensure they're done speaking before you ask your question or make a comment.

Paraphrase what you heard to make sure you're both on the same page. This is especially true if the other person is asking something of you. Clarify your role.

Step 4: Show Appropriate Empathy When Necessary

If this person is telling you his cat died, show proper empathy, even if you're not a cat person. Imagine losing your pet dog or goldfish, think about how you'd feel if you lost something that you cared about.

Don't fake it but imagine yourself in their shoes and act appropriately.

Why Does Communication Matter?

Going forward you can communicate in a new and positive way with your ex: he will see that you have changed. You listen, see his point of view, and then react. It will shock him in a wonderful way. He might respond in the same style. You can talk to each other with respect and assess how you might move forward.

CHAPTER 14

It's Time for Him to Step Off His Pedestal

Your ex may sit high atop a pedestal in your eyes. You have idolized held him in higher regard than he probably deserved. This is especially true after the breakup when your emotions are high and you're feeling lonely.

When you put someone on a pedestal, you magnify his strengths and ignore his weaknesses. You view your relationship with him as unrepeatable. You spend time focusing on the good times. You recall your trip to London and how you rode in the double-decker busses. You remember all the cute little notes he left around the apartment.

Any man can do that for you, and you can take another trip to London or somewhere else with a new guy and it may be even better than this trip you're memorializing. While you're remembering, you conveniently forget about how he constantly forced his plans on your trip, leaving you with things you wanted to do but never got the chance.

So how do you take him off his pedestal?

Evaluate the Good *and* the Bad Traits

Get yourself two separate pieces of paper. On one, write the things about your ex that completely annoyed the heck out of you. Then, write his positive traits. It's helpful to write down your answers, instead of just answering them in your head. Answer these questions:

- What did you like about your ex?
- What did you dislike about him?
- What was great about how he made you feel?
- What was not so great about how he made you feel?
- What was great about your relationship?
- What was not so great about your relationship?

As you examine these positives and negatives, recall the feelings that resulted from his actions, good or bad. When did his actions conflict with your values? When were you frustrated by his words or actions?

How often did you experience these negative feelings? Do you honestly believe that's how someone who loves you should make you feel? Is that the type of relationship you want to have?

Then, examine how you wish your relationship with him was different. If you could change anything about your relationship with your ex, what would it be? Which events or actions didn't meet your expectations?

Try to focus on the bigger things, not the dozens of little things, as the bigger things will add more *umph* to your effort to remove him from his pedestal.

Doing this exercise requires you to be very honest with yourself and you may dredge up some pain while you're doing it, but that's okay. Allow those feelings to flow through you. Don't deny them. Acknowledge that you're angry, sad, or frustrated. Feel it, and then move on.

Now it's time for your second piece of paper. If you already used two, get another. On this second piece of paper, dig into your relationship a little further.

This time, examine things like trust and betrayal. Ask yourself these questions and write down your responses:

- Were there times when you felt you couldn't trust him?
- Did he ever betray you?
- Did you ever feel worried or insecure?
- Did you overlook things because you didn't want to acknowledge them?
- When something came along that was important to you, did you compromise, or did you stand your ground?

- Did you allow things to happen that you shouldn't have?
- When you were a young woman and you envisioned your relationship with your dream guy, did any of it look like what you experienced with your ex?
- Was there ever a feeling that something just wasn't right?
- Being brutally honest with yourself, pinkie swear and all, were there ever moments when you *didn't* see yourself with this guy *forever*?

Now What?

You have a clearer picture of your ex, warts and all. Take a break, especially if it was a very emotional experience for you. Process your emotions. Acknowledge them.

This is not a time to blame yourself for *anything*. Remember that sheet of good stuff? Your relationship wasn't all bad. It's just that the bad stuff probably stirred more uncomfortable emotions and they aren't sitting well.

You have two choices to make, but not right this minute.

Do you still want to get back with your ex or do you want to move forward with these steps and find someone new?

You might not be ready to make that decision yet. In fact, I doubt you're ready and that's okay. I don't expect you to make that call until you're well into building your confidence in Step Three.

If you decide to get back with your ex, you need to deal with some of the issues raised in your evaluation. If he betrayed you, there is a trust issue, and you will need to allow him to rebuild your trust.

If you feel you compromised more and allowed things you wish you hadn't, you need to establish some ground rules and boundaries with him before you consider a new relationship.

If you decide not to get back with your ex, you can use these positives and negatives to determine what type of man you want to be with. Take note of the positive things about your ex and highlight or circle the ones that mean something to you. Make a list to use as a *guideline* when you seek a new relationship.

Also make a list of the stuff that bugged you because those are traits you'll want to avoid in a new partner.

Did You Accomplish Your Goal?

The goal of this chapter was to take your ex down from his pedestal. Have you accomplished that? You didn't set out to demonize him or to have an ex dumping session with a parade of all his negative traits. Hopefully, you found positive and negative things to remember and write down.

CHAPTER 15

Do You Miss Him or Do You Miss Someone?

While you think you miss your ex, you might only miss having someone special in your life, not specifically him.

How can you distinguish between the two?

If You Think About Him When You're Lonely...

If he only comes to mind when you're lonely, you miss being loved, more than you miss your ex. This can sneak up on you when you see other couples who appear to be happy.

You don't miss one specific guy, you miss having someone to cuddle up with, like they do. Feeling lonely is no fun, but neither is being in a bad relationship. If you think about him 24/7, you could say you miss him, but if it's just when you're reminded of being single, you miss *someone*.

If You Miss Going Out on Fancy Dates...

Part of the fun of being part of a couple is getting dressed up for a fancy date. A high-end dinner with your favorite guy is special.

But, if you just miss the going out part and not who you're with, you don't miss *him*, you just miss fancy dates.

Dress up and go somewhere nice. There is nothing wrong with enjoying a dinner by yourself. In fact, it's a very bold, confident move. Sure, it's not the same as being with a guy, but it's something to consider!

If You Want a Cuddle Buddy...

Cuddling is a subtle exchange of affection between two people. It makes you feel protected when his arms are wrapped around you, but if all you're missing is the arms, it's not him you're wanting, but simply the affection itself.

I get it, it's more fun to binge watch *Outlander* with your favorite guy, but does that mean it has to be your ex specifically? Probably not.

If You Miss the Activities You Did Together...

Whether it was watching Netflix together or going out for coffee on Saturday mornings, you miss having someone to do things with. It's easy to miss that routine. There's a sense of safety in the routine things in life, so it's natural to miss those things, but that doesn't mean you're missing the person you did them with.

If You Miss Having Your Texting Buddy...

You sent texts back and forth throughout the day – just short notes about things that were happening or making plans for after work.

Now, your texting buddy is gone, and nobody is regaling you with stories of crazy coworkers and the boss from hell. You aren't receiving those *Good Morning Babe* texts or the *I'll be thinking of you as I drift off to sleep* texts and you miss knowing he's out there thinking about you.

You miss the activities, but not necessarily the person attached to them. Many men will behave in a similar way, so this guy isn't special because he does those things.

If You Miss Having Regular Sex...

Sex with your ex was awesome and it makes perfect sense that you miss it now. This doesn't mean you should have sex with the first guy you meet, but it does indicate that you miss great sex, and not necessarily the partner.

If You Know You're Better Off Without Him...

This is the tell-tale sign that you miss someone, but not your ex. The further into these steps you get and the more you evaluate your relationship, the more likely you are to come to this conclusion.

After all the assessments are over, but perhaps not until you start building your confidence, you may come to this conclusion. This is a dead giveaway that you don't miss your ex, you want someone great to be there for you.

The Bottom Line

The bottom line is that you might feel as if your heart is aching for him, when in reality, you just miss being part of a couple, and that's a very natural feeling to experience. Be patient. Even if you don't miss *him*, you still may decide you want him back and that's fine.

Meanwhile, you have some work to do on yourself, which you'll be starting soon enough. In fact, you could make a case for having started that work already!

Regardless of what you decided in this chapter about missing someone or missing your ex, the answer isn't jumping into another relationship, with him or anyone else, until you complete Step Three.

CHAPTER 16

Is He Healthy Enough and Capable of Love?

The unfortunate truth is that not everyone is mentally healthy enough or capable of love. This doesn't mean they don't want to be in a loving relationship. They probably do, but something is holding them back.

I have a set of questions for you to ask yourself. These will help you determine whether he's healthy enough and capable of love.

1. Does He Make Negative Comments About Women?

Some men just hate women. The proper term for this is misogynist and this type of person isn't capable of true love. It can be tough to pick out a misogynist because they may show the world a different person.

At work, church or school, a misogynist acts as if he can tolerate women. He is kind and loving, but at home, he's volatile and disrespectful.

There is *no way* to be in a relationship with this type of man and **you cannot change him**. The person who will change is you as an attempt to avoid his wrath, but there is no avoiding it because if you change something about yourself to *please* him, he'll find something else to complain about. Here are some signs he's a misogynist:

- He feels he has a *right* to control your thoughts and actions
- He uses the Bible and church to justify his actions, even though the Bible and church do not find this type of behavior acceptable
- He finds your opinions and thoughts to be worthless
- He is charming and kind around people outside the family but at home, you walk on eggshells to keep him from blowing up
- When he doesn't get his way, it's not pretty – he yells, threatens, hits or sulks
- You feel confused when you see his mood shifts from the kind and loving person he shows the outside world to the monster he can be at home
- He's never satisfied, no matter how hard you try to change to be who he claims he wants you to be; you feel guilty and wonder what you can do to please him; you lose faith in yourself

- He gets very jealous when you talk to other men, regardless of who they are; he's very possessive and even acts jealous of time you spend on the children
- His possessiveness might take you away from family and friends; while you need those relationships, you need peace at home more, so you let them go
- You're to blame for *everything* that goes wrong, even if you had nothing to do with it; there's always something, in his eyes, that you could be doing better, and his resulting bad behavior is all your fault
- He gets violent when he doesn't get his way

2. Does He Treat Women as Objects?

How does he speak about women? If all he notices are boobs, butts, and relative hotness, he's objectifying women and isn't capable of love. When one person objectifies another, they don't feel the objectified person is intelligent, doesn't deserve to be treated morally, and is less than human.

This type of person sees women as something to use and leave whatever leftovers there are behind for someone else. And yes, I meant to say some*thing* and not some*one*.

He'll never care one little bit about your wants or needs. He won't be there for you in the tough times and he's not going to suddenly decide to stop. This type of person is not capable of love, and much like the misogynist, you can't change who he is.

3. Has He Been There for You When You Needed Him?

You turned yourself inside out to be there for him when his fifteen-year-old dog died. When his mom was sick with cancer, you helped drive her for her chemo treatments. But, when your car died and you needed a ride, where was he? Either nowhere to be found or too busy to step in and save the day.

A man in love, a man capable of love will be there for you when you need him. Of course, there are the odd times when he truly can't beg out of a meeting with his boss, but he does everything he can to help you solve your problem anyway.

A man who only wants you to meet his needs but doesn't care about yours is not capable of love.

4. Does He Have a History of Abuse and Cheating?

A history of cheating doesn't mean one instance, it is a pattern of behavior. He moves on to a new woman before he's exited his current relationship.

A man in love isn't out looking for someone else to love and a man capable of love doesn't want to exist in shallow relationships.

As far as abuse goes, if you know he's been abusive in the past and you somehow think you're different and he won't abuse you, or you think he won't abuse you when you get back together because he promises not to, you're wrong.

Unless he seeks intensive therapy for his issues, he's going to pick up right where he left off.

Both are signs of major character flaws and signs that he's not mentally healthy enough or capable of love.

5. Is Life with Him a Life of Excuses?

Many people cannot own their behavior, no matter how obvious it is to everyone that they're at fault. This plays out in a couple different ways.

Let's look at an example.

James planned to pick Kate up for their date at seven, but he didn't show, and Kate got worried. She tried texting James, to no avail. There was no reply for hours. Finally, late into the evening, James came up with some excuse about a friend whose old girlfriend showed up and James just had to go there.

Okay, the excuse is lame for starters. Who is more important, the woman he claims to love or the friend? The friend wasn't in any physical danger. He just found a convenient excuse to bail on the date. The second problem is that James could have taken three minutes to text Kate and tell her he was going to help his friend.

Kate and James continue to date for another month or so until he pulls this again. They're planning to go out and again, James is a no-call, no-show. This time, Kate has had enough and when James finally produces another lame excuse, Kate tells him off. What does he do? Instead of apologizing or owning his behavior, he tries to put it on her. He tries to make her feel badly for being angry with him.

This is another way people who can't love function in relationships. Everything is your fault, or the fault of someone else, but never his.

6. Does He View Dating as a Transaction?

You go on a date with a guy, and he pays for dinner. The next thing you know, he expects you to have sex with him, as payment for dinner. He buys dinner, then he gets sex.

When someone like this gets married, the transactions get bigger. If you ask him to watch the kids for an hour so you can run to the grocery store in peace, you owe him that hour in another way. He wants an hour, or more likely three or four hours, with his friends. He bargains for sex or something else he wants.

It's fine to joke around about these things, but when it's the reality of your relationship, you're with someone who doesn't see you as a person. He sees you as a means to his end. He wants sex and he's willing to pay the cost of dinner to get it.

He wants to hang with his friends, so he'll stay home and play video games while he watches the kids.

7. Does He View You as an Accessory?

A man in love doesn't use the woman he's with to boost his ego. When a guy views you as an accessory, it indicates that he is self-centered and that he's only with you because you bring something to the relationship that he thinks he needs to boost his ego.

An example is if you're wealthier than he is, or your job carries status that his does not. He views you as stunningly beautiful or powerful in some way because of these things, and there is something about you that boosts his already over-inflated ego even more. Should you lose your money, your looks, or your job, you won't have any value to him.

Self-centered people surround themselves with people who boost their ego. Look at the woman I snagged! A doctor! See how great I am?!?! Or this beautiful woman is with me! This must mean I'm super important.

Ugh give me a break. This type of guy is not capable of love.

CHAPTER 17

What Was Your Role in the Breakup and How Can You Fix Things?

Nobody is perfect. You are a human being who was created not to be perfect. If you're someone who strives for perfection, this is life-altering news.

Do your best with what you have and know. When you make mistakes, it's either because you aren't equipped with the right tools in a physical way, i.e., not enough money or other resources, or you aren't equipped with knowledge, and this doesn't equate to intelligence.

Mistakes are learning opportunities and not bad things. A mistake is a chance to learn, to do something better the next time, and that's what you're about to do. Learn about mistakes you made because you weren't properly equipped, and then decide what you can learn from that and do better next time.

When you see it like that, it doesn't seem so bad, right? You're about to gain new tools and learn something else. That's good stuff!

Previously, you read that communication is the number one reason for many breakups, but there are a couple of others that float to the top. Another is that you slide into a routine and stop paying enough attention to one another. As you develop a routine, you reach a point where you feel you're happy and your partner is happy, so you stop worrying about your happiness or theirs.

Early in your relationship, you seduced one another, but now you've slipped into routines and there is little to no seduction. That's where your passion, energy and heat came from, and now you don't feel those emotions.

These aren't things you do intentionally and either or both of you can be unintentionally guilty of letting things go.

Examine the errors couples make in their relationships, male and female, and determine if any of these apply to you.

1. You Didn't Pay Enough Attention to One Another

This one happens so easily that you don't realize it's a problem until it's a big problem. When someone feels neglected in a relationship, they think it's petty to bring it up, but it grows and becomes a bigger wound.

This comes in all shapes and sizes. If you doted on your ex and then you had a child, the child will require some of the attention you once placed on your ex. This can be a real problem. The solution is that you both pay attention to your child and to one another, but sometimes that can be a challenge.

This is solved by enjoying regular date nights, at least two a month if not weekly. During date nights, you set aside phones and conversations about mundane things. You connect and share things.

You flirt and act like you did when you were first dating. This time together is so important, especially if one of you feels neglected in the relationship. This is a chance to dress up in that little black number you know he likes. It's also his chance to spend a little time chasing you. Just because you've been together for a while doesn't mean you have to give up that passion and heat. Stir it up with date night!

2. You're Too Negative

Nobody likes to be around someone who is negative all the time. This happens when you lack confidence and self-esteem. You over-analyze everything or have irrational fears about his feelings toward you. It can be exhausting to try to be with someone like this. No matter how many times he tells you he loves you, you're always looking for the *real* truth.

After all, he can't possibly love you because you find yourself undeserving of love. You expect him to reject you which means you may keep your true feelings and opinions to yourself as a way of avoiding that rejection.

In Step Three, you will work on your self-confidence and self-esteem, and you will move past feeling this way. I believe you are worthy of a great relationship with a man who can love every ounce of you from head to toe, but you must believe it too!

3. Your Default Response to His Requests is "No"

We all need freedom to be ourselves, to do things we enjoy and to spend time with people we like. If he asks to hang out with his friends or do things on his own and you tell him he can't, he will become frustrated.

Just because he hangs out with his friends doesn't mean he's looking for a new girlfriend. Going off by himself to enjoy a hobby isn't him leaving you or going off with another woman. Your low self-esteem is telling you you're not worthy of a great guy like him, and your mind plays tricks and tells you these lies.

The answer is to build your confidence. If you're a high-confidence woman who has her act together and a guy leaves you, it's his loss. Once you see relationships in this way, you'll lose this knee-jerk "no" response. You have your own friends to hang out with and your hobbies.

4. You Forget to Compliment Him

We all like to hear we did something well. That doesn't change as we get older. If he's doing things for you, it's a sign of his love. Men are much more likely to act on their love than to say the words *I love you.* Many women misinterpret a man's actions this way. They get frustrated because they don't hear the words and they miss the signals.

When he does something for you, even if it's just taking out the trash or doing the dishes, compliment him on a job well done. Don't overdo it because it's not special then. Time them carefully and mean what you say. An empty compliment is as bad as none.

5. Threatening to Break Up Is Your Usual Mantra

Constantly threatening to break up is manipulative. It's a way to get your partner to do what you want him to do or concede to you in an argument. The worst part of the threat is that it was an idle threat and an empty one. You'd never break up with him because this is a low confidence move and what other man would want you?

Instead, fight fair. A fight is a loud communication where each person is more interested in their own agenda than that of their adversary. Your listening skills play a **bigger** role in settling your disagreement than threatening to break up ever would.

When you're using this as a weapon, at some point, he will break up with you, mostly because he's sick of you threatening to do so.

Ending this behavior requires two things: higher confidence and better communication skills. When you find yourself in a disagreement, rather than continuing, say something like, *"You know, Gregg, we're both a little overheated right now. Let's take a few moments to cool off and then we can try to talk calmly."*

Then walk away and get yourself together. It might take a few moments, or it might take a thirty-minute run but do whatever it takes to burn off the angry energy so you can speak reasonably. You read about this in Step One. You're experiencing a highly emotional moment and you need time to get back to your wise mind.

6. You Tell Lies

You might not see it as a problem to tell him you only spent one-hundred dollars on those new boots when you spent one-hundred fifty dollars, but it is a big deal if you know you need to lie about it. When you lie, you're saying you don't trust him to react in a reasonable way, and you're breaking down the trust in your relationship.

Trust, along with great communication, are two cornerstones of a great relationship. With each lie one of you tells, you chip away at that cornerstone until it's whittled down so much that the structure it was holding up can't stand.

Lies might seem small, but that the person being lied to always finds out and that begets a bigger negative response than if you'd told the truth to begin with.

Other sorts of lies include adhering to the theory that it's better to ask for forgiveness than permission. Wouldn't it have been better to discuss the expensive boots first and talk about how you could save up for them, instead of putting them on the credit card he's trying to pay down?

7. Avoiding Arguments

Another example of poor communication is avoiding arguments. You are not voicing your concerns in a way that allows the two of you to work out a solution.

You fear the outcome, but if you use your listening skills before forming your response, instead of flying off the handle, a disagreement can often be settled.

When you avoid an argument by ignoring the situation, what you're doing is putting blocks in a wall that develops between you. A disagreement means you have differing opinions in an important situation or circumstance. You don't even want to give him the chance to voice his opinion and he will become frustrated. The wall builds because tension and contempt begin to become immovable blocks.

If there is something building between you, take time when you're both feeling good and open it up for discussion. If you become too emotional, step away until you can both calm down, then return with the reminder that listening is your best communication skill. Acknowledge what he needs from you and voice what you need from him, then work out a way for both of you to get what you want.

8. He's the Relationship Workhorse

Relationships are partnerships where two people work together toward common goals. But, when one person is doing everything, it can become a contemptuous situation. He works while you stay home and shop. He cooks, does the dishes, and even goes to the grocery store. When you're spending time together, it's always, *"Honey can you get me…"* or *"Gee do you mind… ."*

Relationships are about give and take. One partner can't always be giving while the other takes. Do the dishes together or if he cooks, you clean up. Get up and get your own soda from the fridge and offer to get him one too. Get a part-time job so you can buy your own shoes.

Make it a goal to do something for your guy once a day. Be mindful of the give and take balance and do your part.

9. You Stuff Your Feelings

Stuffing your feelings down might be a life-long habit for you, so it can be challenging to stop. You think you're being aloof or non-confrontational, but you're stonewalling him and it's not cool. This is a low self-esteem move. You might not believe your feelings are valid or worth energy. Alternatively, you might just be afraid to feel them because you've had a lot of hurt in your past.

Whether your feelings are good or bad, it's important to share them with your partner. If you truly struggle to feel your feelings, you should seek therapy to uncover the reason behind this avoidance.

If you're just afraid that by sharing your feelings, you'll scare him off, that's anxiety and you already read about dealing with anxiety. If you can't share your feelings with your guy, he might not be the right guy for you.

10. You Tried to Change Him

The only person you can change is yourself. Trying to change someone else is not cool and will not work. If he wants to change for you, that's his choice, but forcing him to change will never work. This includes trying to change anything from his wardrobe to his job or friends.

You may do this to improve your own social status or make him into someone you know your family will like. You're afraid your friends will judge him because he's too geeky, so you ask him to get contacts and end the plaid shirt phase of his life, but he won't feel comfortable in your image of him and besides, your friends may find him cute just as he is. If you love him for who he is, the people who are important to you will also, and if they don't, it's their loss.

If he isn't your type, find another guy, but don't make this guy fit a mold that isn't his. You fell for this guy for a reason, as he is, so trying to change him may turn him into someone you don't like. Bet you didn't think of that.

11. You Can't Let Things Go

Chances are you've both done things to annoy or hurt one another. After he's apologized for what he did, your role is to let it go. Forgive and let it pass.

Sometimes, you might hang onto old hurts and bring them up every time something comes up between you.

You have an argument over who's going to take out the dog. Six months ago, he made you take the dog out and you tripped down the steps and sprained your ankle. At this juncture of the current *who's gonna walk the dog* argument, you bring it up… again. You bring it up every time you have a dispute over the dog.

This comes from having some deeply rooted insecurity that's going unaddressed. To stop this behavior, you need to improve your self-esteem and confidence.

Forgiving someone feels as if you're saying what they did was okay, but that isn't what forgiveness is about. When you don't forgive someone, you give space in your mind to anger and bitterness. You allow that person to live rent-free in your head. There is a constant niggling about their infraction that just never goes away.

When you forgive someone, you aren't saying what they did was okay. You're saying that you're letting go of it. You're booting it from your mind with a hefty eviction notice and a big heave-ho. You don't even need to forgive them face-to-face. Maybe you can't. Forgiveness is for you. It's your way of saying you're letting go of the hurt that person caused and you're not harboring ill feelings. It's very freeing.

Think of it this way. Each thing you need to forgive is a heavy rock in the boat that's keeping you afloat in life. As you forgive someone, you toss that rock out of your boat and into the water. Your boat becomes lighter and carries less of a burden. That's how you will feel when you start forgiving. Lighter and unburdened.

12. He's Afraid to Share Things with You

If your ex was always afraid to tell you things because he is fearful that you will fly off the handle before he had a chance to explain, it's a problem.

In each moment of your life, you are making choices on how you will react to something.

People who are reactive fly off the handle without stopping to think about their reaction and the impact it may have.

This is another low confidence move and it shows a lack of self-control.

If your ex comes in and tells you he lost his job, your first response shouldn't be to fly off the handle about how irresponsible he is, blah blah blah. Your first response should be empathy and kindness. If you take the time to stop and think about your reply first, you will likely choose a different one.

13. You're Wishy-Washy

Nothing is more aggravating than to ask someone their opinion and have them get wishy-washy on you.

> *Where would you like to have dinner tonight?*
>
> *Ohhhh...I don't know.*
>
> *Come on now, my treat. Where are we going!*
>
> *I can't decide...you choose.*

Men **hate** this conversation. He asked you where you want to go because he wants to please you and you just tossed it back in his face. Now, he's going to choose and he's going to go to that Asian fusion place he likes and you don't. Then you become angry because he didn't go somewhere you like.

Well...you had a choice, and you gave up that choice so now you get to suck it up and deal. If someone asks your opinion on something, provide it. Not doing so is a low confidence move. You're afraid if you say where you want to go, *he* will get upset.

He knows you may choose something he doesn't like, but he's willing to take the chance to make you happy. All that happened out of a nice gesture he was trying to make was that he got to eat food he liked, and you got ticked. That wasn't the outcome he was going for.

14. You Humiliate Him or You Don't Have His Back

I've seen couples do this, and it's ugly. Let's imagine you and your guy are at a party. He is hanging out with some of the guys, but he's within a distance to overhear your conversation. You're sharing something with your girlfriends that happened between the two of you and you say something demeaning about your ex, like saying he was dumb or looked like crap, or anything similar to this.

When he hears this he will be humiliated, of course. If he could hear your conversation, so could his friends, not to mention the friends you said it to directly. How can he stay at this party any longer without feeling embarrassed and humiliated? This is just plain mean and not at all funny, which is how you may have thought it would come off. This is bullying.

When people do this, they feel badly about themselves. The way they choose to feel better is to make someone else feel worse. Build your confidence and you'll be less inclined to make others feel miserable.

The other piece of this is not having his back. Let's imagine you're at a family get together and your Aunt Bessy, who is nearly deaf, yells to your mom who's sitting next to her that your guy needs to lop off twenty pounds. Of course, everyone in the room just heard her, including your guy, who is now trying to hide his embarrassment.

If you have his back, you'll give Aunt Bessy a bit of a talking to about her rude remark, and you'll be sure to let her know that you love your guy, warts and all. If you don't have his back, you'll either ignore her or chime in with something like, "*Yeah I've been trying to get him to lose weight, but he just won't listen.*"

Being in a relationship should make you feel safe and secure, but if you *don't* have his back, or if you bully and humiliate him in front of others, he's not feeling very safe and secure, and he sure isn't feeling loved.

Now What?

If any of this sounds like you, there are things you can do. Most of them involve working your way carefully through Step Three and rebuilding your confidence. When your confidence and self-esteem are low, it has an impact on every other area of your life and while you can be very confident in some areas of your life and not very confident in others, self-esteem is all-encompassing.

Once you relearn how to place value on yourself and you learn that you are capable of more than you thought, many of these behaviors will fall off your radar naturally.

CHAPTER 18

How Do I Know When I'm Ready for Step 3?

You are ready for Step Three when you have fully assessed your relationship, including any role you may have played. You have removed him from his pedestal, and you see him for who he truly is, for better or worse. You have a better understanding of what he's thinking and feeling right now as well.

You also recognize what's behind the lies he told you about the breakup and you're aware that some of them mean he might not want to come back. The time to assess whether you want him back will come later.

You understand the difference between missing him and missing having someone in your life. This helps you to put your feelings about the breakup into perspective.

You have read about whether he's mentally healthy and capable of love and you know that if you're continuing, it's because he doesn't exhibit any of those signs.

This Step was a bit of a tough one as you had to dig through some crap to work through it but be proud of yourself for completing this step! It's not fun to evaluate something for what was good and bad about it. It's more fun to assess the good and forget the bad, but knowledge is power and you're stronger for the work you've done!

To restate, you're ready to move on to Step 3 when:

- You've checked all the boxes in Are You Ready to Move on to Step Two
- You have taken him down from his pedestal and you see both the positive and negative traits he has
- You understand the lies he told, and you see that some of those lies indicate he won't be coming back
- You've sorted out your feelings over missing him versus missing having someone in your life
- You've assessed whether he's capable of love and you've determined he is
- You have evaluated the possible things you did wrong and you're ready to correct them by working your way through Step Three

step 3

Rebuilding Your Confidence

Many women want to skip this step. *"It's boring. I don't need this. I just want him back."*

What would happen if I told you to walk over to a handsome man across the room and engage him in stimulating conversation? Would you do it comfortably or would you freeze up?

Somewhere along the road of life, you either didn't build much confidence or something happened to lower your confidence. Regardless of the reason, that's about to change.

Confident women live outside their comfort zone. They fail, laugh at their failures, learn, and succeed the next time. They have goals, a vision of what they want in life, and a path to get there. They have boundaries. They become students and are never victims. They are happy and positive.

They attract men.

And yes, they can impress their ex-boyfriends to the point where they have no choice but to beg forgiveness and return!

If you've overcome your emotions and you've honestly assessed your relationship with your ex, you're ready to move on to this third step, rebuilding your confidence.

Your confidence took a nosedive after the breakup, partly because he lied about the reasons for the breakup.

You discovered you had a role in the breakup as well and that's a hard pill to swallow. Breakups are rarely the fault of one person and now, you're beating yourself up over it.

It's time to end the blame game all around and start rebuilding your confidence. **Great men are attracted to confident women**. He was attracted to your confidence when you met, unless neither of you had confidence, in which case, your relationship was probably co-dependent. Either way, it's time to build *your* confidence.

Rebuilding your confidence puts you in the power position in this reconciliation! YOU hold the key to getting back together once you've rebuilt your confidence.

Right now, your confidence is lower than you think it is. Having time when you aren't in a relationship allows you to rebuild it without the distractions that come with being in a one.

Many things happened during your relationship to help this process along. You gave up part of yourself to please your partner. If there was something you enjoyed, like scuba diving, but he didn't, you probably gave that up. Now, you can pursue it again and maybe this time, you can get him excited about learning it or at least encourage him to give it a try.

Nurturing women tend to over-nurture their man, especially if he's going through a difficult time. While a man will go along with this for a short time, most men don't like to be nurtured 24/7, so that nurturing nature of yours needs to be focused on something else, like a puppy or a goldfish.

This step is all about you. You will learn a lot of great things about yourself, and you will feel 1000% better by the time you get to the end of the step.

In this step, you will learn:

- The importance of being an independent woman, what that means and how to get there
- How to make positive changes in your life, what that means and why it's so important
- Why it's time to break your routine and how It will help in your quest to get him back
- The importance of self-care and how to implement a self-care routine into your life
- How to create a vision board and start living the life you dream of
- Why you need a story and how to write yours
- How to stop living in the past
- The difference between being a student and a victim and now to transition from victim to student

CHAPTER 19

Being a Truly Independent Woman

I must confess that this chapter is borrowed from my confidence course, *Build Yourself and He Will Come*. The lesson is powerful and worth repeating!

Dependence vs. Independence vs. Interdependence

Every day, I receive emails from women who share their relationship frustrations. Sometimes, it's an instance of a woman being in a relationship with men who are not yet mature enough in their mental development to be worthy of a great woman. They are what women might call leaches, losers, slackers, worthless bums, etc. I like wet kittens.

Often, however, the emails I receive go something like this:

> *"Joe and I have been dating for a while now and I thought we were really in love. We do everything together. I can't*

> *remember a time when I was apart from him. We seemed like we were in sync with one another. I gave him everything he wanted. I took care of him. I did his laundry, cleaned his apartment, and even walked his dog if he had a long workday. Recently, though, he's been distant. He doesn't call or text every day like he used to. He seems like he is pulling away and I don't understand why. I think he might be seeing someone else! I'm so depressed because I don't know what to do! Everything I try seems to just make things worse. I tried showing up where I know he's hanging out with his friends but, even then he is distant. What can I do? I am afraid he's seeing someone else! Help!!!"*

Or this…

> *"Gregg, I don't know what to do. Steve packed up all his things last week and moved out! One day, it seemed like we were clicking and the next, he's gone. I feel so lost without him. I just sit and cry when I'm home and he's not here. My friends all have their own boyfriends and they're too busy to come over. I found an old shirt of his and I keep it under my pillow so I can still smell him near me. I thought we were in love. I thought he was the one. Gregg, PLEASE help me get him back! I'm desperate!"*

There are a few other varieties, but the underlying problem remains the same, as does my advice. What I find is that women are usually very reluctant to follow my advice. I want to take this chapter to explain what this advice is and why it is so vital for you to take it.

Dependence

From the time we are born until we reach our teen years, we are primarily dependent on our parents for just about everything. We earn an allowance which enables us to buy that treasured game or toy we've had our eye on but, overall, we rely on them for everything. As we grow into teens, hopefully our parents have molded a sense of independence and responsibility into us. We begin to learn the value of hard work, having money and learning new things. Sometimes this happens and sometimes it does not.

In a dependent relationship, you give up your own needs for the needs of your partner. This is not a healthy relationship. To understand dependence, let's look at a few examples.

Jennifer

When Jennifer and Mark met, it was pure magic. Within a few weeks, Jennifer stopped going to the Thursday night Girl's Night outings, she stopped going to Yoga class and she barely ever called her best friend, Emily, just to chat and catch up. She didn't even do her favorite thing anymore – painting. Mark was her whole world. She loved everything about him.

Mark, however, is in a different place. He wants to hang out with his friends, go jet-skiing on the weekends and spend hours at the gym working out. When she complains about him spending time away, he grows distant, and Jennifer becomes depressed. The more distant he becomes, the more depressed and anxious about the relationship she becomes.

Then, he calls or texts, wanting to hang out. Jennifer's mood immediately improves and for a couple weeks, things seem to be back on track. Jennifer is happy again because Mark seems to love her after all. The very next time he doesn't text when he should or declines to hang out, Jen is right back where she was before – depressed and anxious. She's sure this time, the relationship is over.

WHAT HAPPENED?

Jennifer gave up everything to be Mark's girlfriend. Her entire sense of happiness was wrapped up in the actions of Mark. With him gone, she was unhappy. If he didn't text or call, she was miserable and sure the relationship was over. When he was around, she was happy and thought things were on the right track. Jennifer had become dependent on Mark for her very happiness instead of seeking it in hanging out with friends and doing the things she loved.

Madeline

Madeline is a successful woman. She graduated from college, got a job in a hospital as a physical therapist and has a great group of friends. She wasn't afraid to go see a movie by herself or go out to dinner alone if nobody was available. Then, Maddy met Josh and fell in love, possibly for the first time ever. She wanted to do everything with Josh. If Josh didn't want to go to a movie, she didn't go, no matter how badly she wanted to see the film. If he didn't want to have Chinese for dinner, rather than go by herself, she would cave in and do what he wanted to do. Maddy felt miserable but she couldn't really pinpoint why. She was in love – this was supposed to feel great! Why didn't it?

WHAT HAPPENED?

Madeline was so happy when she was with Josh that she began to believe she couldn't be happy if she was apart from him. She lost her identity as Maddy and became Josh's girlfriend. The once fiercely independent Madeline became dependent on Josh for her happiness.

Sabrina

Sabrina and Matt met through mutual friends. They hit off and started dating but now, Matt's true personality is shining through. Matt loves to go out drinking with his buddies and doesn't communicate with Sabrina for days. When he's around, he puts her down or compares her to other women. He tells lies about her to his friends and treats her like crap. After a few months, Sabrina broke it off. How can she like such a jerk?

A week into the breakup, Sabrina is miserable. She is so lonely and lost without Matt. Even though their relationship is just a few months old, she misses him, so when he comes crawling back a month later, she takes him back, even though she knows he will make her miserable. She feels happy again on some level because she has a man in her life – any man. This relationship meets its demise again and Sabrina meets another guy who is Matt in a different man's body. The same patterns emerge, and she breaks it off, only to take him back as well. A few losers later, Sabrina sees a pattern, but she doesn't know what to do.

WHAT HAPPENED?

Sabrina snagged a wet kitten, but being low on confidence herself, she believes all of Matt's put-downs, rather than seeing them for what they are – his attempt to make her feel as badly about herself as he feels about himself. She feels she would rather be in a relationship – any relationship - than be alone. After all, who knows when another guy will show interest in her? If she isn't in a relationship, she is unhappy. Her happiness is wrapped up in whether she is in any relationship.

Trish

Trish feels anxious all the time now. She's in a great relationship with Dan and things are going great – that is if she knows where he is and what he's doing. When Dan is at work or out with his friends, her anxiety becomes almost unbearable. What is he doing? Who is he with? Are other women flirting with him? Is that jerk Jon introducing him to girls? She's a mess. She sneaks around to check on Dan, you know – to see if he's where he said he would be. She has even gone as far as putting on a wig to make sure he isn't hanging out with other women.

When Dan is with Trish, she feels so much relief. She can relax because she knows what he's doing and who he's doing it with. She can control things much easier when she is there to keep tabs on him. Dan, meanwhile, is growing more and more tired of Trish's antics. He's seen her hanging out in the corner of the bar, wearing that ridiculous wig and he's about had enough. He feels smothered and as if he isn't trusted. Dan is pretty much done with Trish.

WHAT HAPPENED?

Trish's own low self-esteem makes her want to control everything about Dan. She feels if she isn't in control of what he's doing, she will lose him. She feels anxious all the time, instead of feeling happy and fulfilled. Yet, she is so dependent on her need to control the situation that she can't see how miserable she truly is. Dan, on the other hand, sees through her control and he's ready to snap like he's been fired out of a slingshot. Her controlling and neediness drove him away. Due to her distrust, he wants to be away from her more and more – the very thing she is trying to prevent.

Eve

Eve met Paul at a bookstore while looking for a cookbook on Mediterranean food. She notices him watching her, so he introduces himself and they hit it off. He shares that his grandmother was an excellent good cook. Since Eve is totally into cooking, she feels they are totally in sync. They see each other more and more frequently until they are inseparable.

The problem is Paul is relying more and more on Eve for… well for everything. Turns out Paul is in between jobs and needs a place to stay until he gets back on his feet again. Now he lays around all day on Eve's couch while she works. She comes home to whatever mess of dishes and dirty clothes he's left around and his expectation of a home cooked meal. Eve doesn't mind. He needs her to take care of him! Over time, Eve becomes more like Paul's mother than his girlfriend. Meanwhile, her own needs are going unmet. She's exhausted and he's sucking not only her bank account but her energy.

WHAT HAPPENED?

Eve likes the feeling of taking care of someone. She is a nurturer and desperately wants children. In lieu of children, she has Paul, who is very accepting of the nurturing – too accepting. He loves having someone take care of him because it means he can continue in his wet kitten ways of taking advantage of her. Eve is Paul's caregiver. She's dependent on him to make her feel needed and he is dependent on her for, well – everything.

Sarah

Sarah went through school basically hating herself. She doesn't like the clothes she wears; she hates her hairstyle, and she sucks at putting on makeup, so she doesn't bother. She was raised by her mother who works two jobs to support Sarah and her brother. When her mother comes home, she's tired and cranky, often snapping at Sarah for not doing one thing or another right. Her mother has a specific way she wants things to be done and she doesn't like it when her standards aren't met. Sarah never shows any interest in boys in school because she assumes none of them want to date her. She allowed herself to become overweight and she really doesn't care. She does have one thing going for her – she loves animals. After all, animals love you back no matter what!

Enter Brian. Brian shows interest in Sarah. He sees through her weight to a sensitive woman. He likes how careful she is and how caring she is toward animals, especially since he loves animals so much himself. As they date, their flaws begin to shine, and problems develop. Brian is a control freak, and he wants to control everything Sarah does. Since this is how she grew up, she doesn't think much of it. Sarah conforms to Brian's every whim and if Brian is happy, Sarah thinks she's happy. The truth is, she isn't.

WHAT HAPPENED?

Because Sarah doesn't hold herself to high standards, neither does Brian. Sarah has no self-respect, no confidence. Life has beaten her up from a young age. She has a mother who is overworked and tired and never takes the time to help Sarah develop independence in the right way. She is critical and makes Sarah feel as if she can't do anything right. Sarah is so grateful when Brian shows interest, that she doesn't care how he treats her. No other man has ever shown interest in her and she isn't about to get rid of him. Besides, the way Brian treats Sarah is comfortable and familiar to her.

What Do They All Have in Common?

All these relationships have one thing in common: they are relationships built upon dependence, rather than on mutual love and respect. One or both individuals in these relationship examples are dependent on the other for their happiness and sense of fulfillment. A relationship where one or both parties are dependent will never work. When happiness relies on another person, whether it's the mood of the other person or the presence of the other person, the relationship is doomed to fail, as it should.

Dependence on someone else means you have lost, or never gained your own independence. These situations arise when your self-respect and confidence are so low that you are grateful to be in any relationship, whether it's healthy or not. If you're in a relationship with someone who is also low on self-respect and confidence, the result can be one hot mess. Somewhere along the way, I get the email.

Independence

I don't know how to sugar-coat this, so I'm just going to lay it down, right here. You cannot become one-half of a successful relationship until you become an independent, confident woman with high self-esteem and high confidence. No way, no how. To take it further, you cannot easily become an independent woman while you are in a relationship – especially an unhealthy relationship. Why?

Because to become independent, you must get to know yourself from the inside out, and you cannot do this while you are in a relationship. You will always be looking at yourself through the lens of how you want your partner to see you. To grow yourself, you need to be single or at least take a significant relationship break. When women are in relationships, I coach them to tell their partner that they need a few weeks to work on themselves. A partner who truly loves you will give you this time and respect your wishes. A partner who is a wet kitten and unworthy of you will continue to badger you during this time – afraid he is losing you. Keep that in mind as we proceed. How do you become independent?

Get to Know Yourself

You probably think you know yourself, but if you're here, I'm guessing you don't know yourself as well as you should. Getting to know yourself isn't as challenging as you might think. One great activity is journaling every evening. Write down what happened throughout your day and how you feel about it. Don't spend a lot of time thinking about your words. Let them flow.

For example, your sister called and asked you to babysit at the last minute so she could go shopping for a new dress. You said yes, even though it meant canceling your plans. When you journal, write about how you felt about this decision. Were you okay canceling your plans or are you mad at yourself for doing so? If you were okay with it, fine, but if you're mad at yourself, you need to make a change. Next time, you need to be stronger, "Gee Em, I'd really like to help you out tonight, but I have plans with Jessie and the girls. Can you go tomorrow? I'd be happy to watch the kids for you then."

When you journal your day, look at whether you present the same you to the world as the you who lives inside. Sometimes we try to portray someone we are not so we can feel accepted. You may want to fit in with a group at work who always go out to lunch at a place around the corner, so you go, even though you're trying to save money and eat healthy. When you journal, look at how those two things conflicted. To become more independent, you will need to be able to identify what you want and be able to pursue it. "Gee guys, I'd love to go to lunch with you today, but I promised myself I'd eat healthier, so I think I'll pass." This will also keep them from tempting you regularly.

Challenge What You Think You Believe

It is easier to live with the status quo, whatever it is, than to try and stir things up. We often react to situations and types of people out of habit, rather than considering our own beliefs. This causes us to live a life that is outside of what we truly want or value. This can be especially true if you're in a co-dependent relationship. You sacrificed your own beliefs for the beliefs of your significant other, to ensure the relationship wouldn't be in jeopardy.

Take time, now that you are single, to really evaluate what you believe. Do you believe something because it aligns with your own value system or do you believe in it because your friends, parents or a significant other believes in it? This is the time to uncover what your values are and realign your life to be more in tune with them (hint: this is where happiness gets its roots!).

After you evaluate what you believe, challenge those beliefs. Take an honest look at whether what you believe is true or false. Let's look at an example:

> *Belief:* People in control hurt other people with their control. ⇨ People in control don't care about the people they control. ⇨ People in control are really out of control.
>
> *What this means to me:* I don't take control of my life because I fear being out of control – but – I am already out of control. ⇨ I need to take control of my choices. I need to control my actions. I need to let go of misguided beliefs.

Here is another.

> *Belief:* Powerful people are putting on a show. ⇨ Powerful people can't be trusted. ⇨ Powerful people hurt other people.
>
> *What this means to me:* I have been hurt many times by people who hold power over me in some way. I don't trust power – it ruins you. I am derailing my own life by not being powerful.

When you dig into the root of your beliefs –people in control are out of control or powerful people hurt other people, you can look at whether this is really true. Often, these beliefs come from how you've been treated or what you've been raised to believe. When you honestly look at these beliefs, you can begin to see that they are not true at all, but you're using them as excuses not to act in your own life.

Learn to Speak Up for Yourself

Too often, when life beats you down, you become too compliant. You agree to something rather than speak up for yourself. When you don't establish boundaries, people use you and make you feel badly. Being assertive is not easy at first, but once you feel the freedom and happiness of setting and maintaining healthy boundaries and standing up for yourself, you get better at it.

You may be afraid to establish boundaries; you think it makes you seem unavailable or mean, but in truth, people respect you more when you have boundaries. You are someone who respects yourself and it shows. Others won't respect you until you respect you.

Become a Decision-Maker

Men hate this conversation:

> Man: *"Where do you want to go for dinner tonight?"*
>
> Woman: *"Ohhhhhhh, I don't know…."*
>
> Man: *"How about that new fusion place on 5th?"*
>
> Woman: *"Nooooooo…"*
>
> Man: (sighing under his breath) *"Okay then how about that Mexican place in The Square – the one that has the fajitas you like"*
>
> Woman: *"No, I don't feel like Mexican tonight"*
>
> Man: (nearly growling) *"Well what do you feel like then?"*
>
> Woman: *"It doesn't matter. You decide."*

A smart man knows at this point that no matter what he chooses, he loses. He wants you to tell him what you want to do, even if it's not his favorite, he doesn't care. He asked and you need to decide.

Not being able to decide on anything is another low-confidence red flag. Expressing what you really want doesn't make you difficult, it simply means you are someone who knows what she wants and isn't afraid to say so. If you're not sure, follow your values and your passions. One or the other will be appropriate and will guide you.

Set Goals – Have a Plan

Independent people have goals and plans to achieve those goals. They know what they want, and they have a road map to get there. Goals help you look at your future and make the changes you want to make. They help you identify what you want out of life.

When you achieve your goals, your confidence gets a boost. You respect yourself a little more and you walk a little taller. You can set a more difficult goal because you feel this new level of self-esteem. The more difficult you perceive the goal to be, the bigger boost your confidence will get when you reach it.

Develop New Habits

This new, independent version of you is going to need new habits. You're out there now, doing more things, meeting new people, exploring the world through a new set of eyes. You may decide to pursue a healthier lifestyle. This requires a definite change in habits.

Tracking your progress as you develop new habits empowers you to keep going. When I am working on a new habit, I mark the calendar each day I do that new thing. There quickly comes a point when I don't want to miss the chance to put another mark on the calendar! I don't want to start over. It is motivational!

Learn to Take Care of You

Mothers are particularly bad at this. You become a mom and the needs of your children supersede your own. You are so busy taking care of the people in your life that you put taking care of yourself on the back burner. If you aren't taking care of yourself, you're no good for anyone else.

Put more of a priority on taking care of yourself. You do deserve it, regardless of what your low self-esteem is telling you. You are important and you need to take time out to be good to yourself. Dress in clothing that fits – clothing you like. Get a haircut in a style you like. Buy some makeup and let the lady at the counter teach you how to apply it. Get a personal trainer. Do whatever it takes to take care of you and show others that you care about the image you present.

Soothe Yourself

Do you stuff your emotions or ignore them? If so, you don't allow yourself to feel anything because it's uncomfortable. Feeling anxious brings on physical symptoms you don't like.

Feeling sad can make you want to soothe yourself with food, drugs, or alcohol. You don't know how to accept and allow your feelings to happen.

The best way to do this is to label your emotions. When you find yourself wrapped up in an emotional state, label it. It's difficult to deal with emotion if you don't know what you're experiencing. Once you identify the emotion, feel it. If you're sad, feel sad, but don't overdo it. You can go too far the other way. Set a time limit – I will feel sad over Brad moving out today but tomorrow, I'm going to the gym!

Take Some Risks

Risk-taking helps you grow and become more confident. With confidence comes independence.

What makes something risky depends on you. Usually, the things you find risky are things you fear, so start by identifying your fears. Facing them is taking a risk. Each time you do it, the benefits are huge!

Don't Always Seek Agreement

There are two sides to this one. If you always agree with others, it means that you don't have your own opinions, and this makes you agreeable, of course, but it also means you are not independent. You're not doing any of the things you've learned so far.

Equally important is when everyone agrees with you – all the time. Then you're not being independent. You're saying what you think others want to hear. Independent people speak their mind, kindly, and they have opinions. (Men LOVE this!)

Why Independence is SO Important

The only way to interdependence, also known as a healthy relationship, is through independence. You cannot enter a healthy relationship if you're dependent. When you're dependent, the only relationship option is co-dependence, which is an unhealthy relationship. The last section of this chapter is about interdependence. That's what you're shooting for.

I hope you can see why it is easiest to find independence when you are single and why it is so important. Men like women who:

- Can make decisions
- Have opinions
- Have interests outside of the relationship
- Set clear boundaries and don't break them – for anyone
- Are challenging because they are busy and always learning new things
- Have high confidence and self-esteem
- Are mysterious because they're always doing something new and interesting
- Have goals and enjoy rising to meet challenges
- Are willing to take risks

Interdependence

The difference between interdependence and co-dependence seems fuzzy, but hopefully not for long. You aren't going to spend a lot of time on interdependence because your focus is on becoming independent, but it's crucial to understand the difference and the importance of your journeys.

Co-Dependence vs. Interdependence

Dana and James have been together since college. They met at an on-campus charity event for cancer, and they immediately hit it off. James graduated a couple of quarters before Dana and found a job soon after. He saved and soon was in a nice apartment. He maintained a couple of friendships from college and had some good friends from his high school days. He loved hanging out with his friends, but he also loved hanging out with Dana.

Dana graduated and got a job as well. It took her a little longer because she wanted to stay in the same area as James, but she got a job and her own apartment nearby. She fell in love with horseback riding as a young girl and now that she didn't need to study all the time, she enjoyed riding again. She also took a few art classes in college and began to pursue that as a hobby. She did a girl's night every couple of weeks with some of her friends from college and had a great life on her own. When she and James were together, they both felt happy and fulfilled.

As time passed, James and Dana talked about their future. James figured out that while he enjoys hanging out with his friends, he really loves being with Dana. She doesn't complain about his guy time when he wants it and she still surprises him in little ways, like the day she announced they were going hiking for the day or the time she brought him a big bowl of his favorite soup, the kind his mom always got him, when he wasn't feeling well. Dana is always up to something, and he loves finding out what her latest thing is. She's mysterious and challenging to him.

James and Dana have an interdependent relationship. Neither of them sacrifices themselves for the sake of the relationship. They work together on the big stuff like where to go on their honeymoon or which neighborhood they'll move into when they buy their first house together. They allow one another the space to remain independent but understand the value of building their own foundation as a couple. Their relationship is balanced and healthy.

From Independent to Interdependent

Once you become an independent, confident woman, you will be choosing men, not grateful to be chosen. You will send men packing left and right! Men are naturally drawn to confident women. The mannerisms of confident women are different, and men are tuned in to those things. Obviously, you'll need a man for an interdependent relationship. Following are characteristics of interdependent relationships.

Both Individuals Have Boundaries

Boundaries are important for an interdependent couple. What does this look like in a relationship?

Mike and Sami recently started dating. Mike has two children from a previous marriage, and he is deeply committed to maintaining a strong relationship with his kids. He has them fifty percent of the time as part of the custody arrangement. Mike has boundaries where his kids are concerned. When his kids are in his care, he doesn't go out on the town or spend a lot of time away from home, other than work of course. He feels it is important to be there when his kids are. He has the time when they're with their mom to do his own thing. He doesn't introduce his kids to a woman he's in a relationship with until he is sure he wants to be with her. This is a boundary for Mike and Sami is fine with it. She loves kids and can't wait to meet his, but she is willing to do so in his time frame.

Maintain Your Uniqueness

One of the things that attracts your guy to you is your uniqueness. There is something about you that makes you shine brighter than the other women he's met. Both of you must maintain your uniqueness. Yes, you will have similarities and as your relationship grows, you will become more alike in some ways, but if you like wearing boho style outfits now, keep on wearing them. If he really doesn't like your style, he wouldn't be interested in the first place.

You must let go of the desire to ditch his favorite Hawaiian shirt. This is part of his uniqueness, and you need to let it be. If it's bad enough, you can jokingly say something like, *"Josh, really with the Hawaiian shirt? Let's look into getting you a new one soon, okay?"* Do this with a wink and a smile so he doesn't think you're just being mean.

Find and Foster Common Ground

In the example of interdependence above, you read that they met at a cancer charity event. This is common ground. There are many ways you can find common ground. You can do it through shared hobbies or things you're both passionate about, such as charitable causes, animals, etc. When you have common ground, it strengthens into the relationship. Your shared experiences and memories build a strong foundation.

Keep the Lines of Communication Open

Communication is key to the success of any relationship. Know when to walk away from a situation, give it time to settle, and come back later in a calmer state, ready to talk and listen.

In The Power to Communicate, which you can get for free at the front of this book, you learn numerous communication tools designed to help you communicate effectively with anyone and come out of the conversation with what you wanted. Too many times, communication fails because it involves not only speaking but listening. You spend a lot of time making sure you're heard, but forget to hear the other person's side or form an empathetic point of view.

Marie wants Chris to fix the bathroom shower this weekend. Rather than badgering him about it, she takes a different approach. *"Chris I was wondering...if I mow the lawn Saturday morning, do you think you could work on our shower? I'll get the parts you need so everything will be ready. I know you've been busy at work, but I really need your expert skills to get the shower fixed right."*

See what she did there? She took on one of his usual chores so he wouldn't feel like she was piling on. She offered to get what he needs to do the job, and she complimented him on his skills. If he fails to do the shower this weekend, her next move is to say something like this, *"I'm going to call Jodi's friend Bill, the plumber and have him come over this weekend to fix the shower."* Bang. Done. Chris will be fixing the shower this weekend.

Respond to One Another's Needs

While your relationship is interdependent, that doesn't always mean your needs will be equal. One of you may have an immediate need which supersedes the other. Illnesses and family emergencies come along and must be dealt with. Rather than stomping around or sulking when your partner has needs greater than your own, step in and be supportive. Find out where you can be of assistance. Do travel arrangements need to be made? Does someone need to be taken to the doctor? How can you step up and help?

Recognize and Adapt to Change

The woman you are today, regardless of how old you are, is not the woman you will be in five or ten years. This goes for men as well. Everyone continues to grow and. You need to allow your partner to grow and evolve. In a positive, interdependent relationship, you consult with one another when big changes come along. If someone is offered a job promotion that would force the family to move to a new city, both must discuss and come to some understanding. Remain open to the desires and concerns of the other.

It's natural to be resistant to change and dig in your heels if someone tries to force change on you, but change is difficult for everyone, not just you. Be supportive of the decision you come to together.

Become Tolerant

We all fall off life's wagon from time to time. Life hits you with something, and you take a nosedive. For men, this can be the loss of a loved one, the loss of a job or not getting a promotion or a host of other events which challenge his natural need to provide or his emotions. It is during a stressful time for a man that a woman often wants to kick in and nurture. This is the farthest thing from what he wants or needs.

A man in any of these situations needs to be left alone until he is ready to talk. He doesn't want to be followed around or badgered with well-intended nurturing. He wants to retreat to his man cave or to his friends until he can sort it out. Your job during this time is to let him be. Recognize his need for space and do your own thing. Take a class in something, go shopping, hang out with your friends or whatever but do your own thing and leave him alone.

Don't immediately jump into *"He's seeing someone I just know it"* and don't let your friends go there either. When a man is emotionally struggling, he needs you to be understanding, tolerant and out of his space until he emerges, ready to talk or ready to move on with life as it was before. If he wants to talk, he will. If he needs your help, he'll ask.

CHAPTER 20

How to Make Positive Changes in Your Life

Are you ready to make positive changes in your life? Are you ready to do the work to make those changes?

Making positive changes in your life doesn't come by magic. There is no pill you can take to suddenly make all of this happen. You must be willing to do the work. The reward is well worth your effort! What is that reward?

- Happiness
- Fulfillment
- Lower anxiety and stress
- Being attractive to men
- Owning the feeling that you can conquer the world
- Feeling strong and powerful
- Feeling in control of your life
- So. Much. More.

The best way to make positive changes is to be methodical, but to approach it at a slow and steady pace. The things you'll learn in this chapter can't be done overnight. Many require you to ditch old habits and form new habits. This takes up to two months.

Develop Healthy Habits

One of the first things to consider is developing healthy habits. This isn't all about working out; it can mean anything from implementing a better sleep schedule to eating healthier meals. If you smoke or use recreational drugs, however infrequent, change that too. This is another thing that you can change to develop healthier habits in your life.

Good health is a gift that you can give to yourself. It's self-respect at its core. When you respect yourself, you want to take care of yourself.

Some other healthy habits include learning how to manage stress and anxiety, which can really have a negative impact on your body if you experience them long-term.

While you're thinking of taking care of yourself, don't forget that self-care routine. Allow yourself time to do something you enjoy. It's a great way to take care of yourself. What this looks like to you will be different than what it looks like to me, so you must figure that part out for yourself.

What do You Want to Change?

What do you want to change? If you see yourself in any of those reasons you may be responsible for the breakup, those might be high on your list.

Are you tired of being a doormat? Setting boundaries might be a great place to start. If you're sick of your job and want another one, what can you do to make that happen? Do you need to take some classes or gain some sort of certification?

Consider all areas of your life. Are you happy with your group of friends? The people to surround yourself with are positive-minded people who encourage you to be your best and don't spend time putting you or others down. They are your support system and you theirs. They have your back no matter what.

Changes can be cosmetic. Do you want a new hair style or color? Do you want to change your wardrobe style? Maybe you want a different home or car. Make a list of the things you want to change, no matter how far out there it seems.

If you get stuck, identify your core values. These help you see why you want to make some of those changes. In fact, the changes you make should align with your values. This helps you move closer to them.

Reprogram Your Mind to Stay Positive

This one is tricky. You're probably saying, *"Gee Gregg if I could do that, I wouldn't need this book!"* Right, I get it, but let's look at how you can do this.

Keep a Gratitude Journal

When things look bleak, turn to what you have in your life to be grateful for. There is always something. During COVID, you may have been grateful for toilet paper! Make a habit of writing in your gratitude journal at least once a day, more if you feel negativity creeping in.

Create and Repeat Positive Affirmations

- I don't need to make others feel badly to feel great about myself
- I am a strong, capable woman
- I can do anything I set my mind to
- I give myself permission to go after whatever I want

Those are just examples. The trick to affirmations is to say them whether you believe them or not. The challenge comes when your confidence or self-esteem are so low that you can't get to that place. If you're battling depression so severe that you don't want to get out of bed most days, you should seek professional help. The same holds true if your confidence and self-esteem are low.

Affirmations take time, patience and observation. Learn how to observe your own thoughts and change them. You'll catch yourself saying things like:

- I can't believe I was so dumb
- I'm such an idiot…
- I'm too fat
- I'm too ugly
- I'll never amount to anything

Your negative thoughts will be different from those. Focus on kicking them out of your mind. When you say, *"I can't believe I was so dumb,"* tell yourself this instead, *"I know I can do a great job"* or whatever fits the situation.

If this isn't sinking in yet, let me ask you this question…would you speak to your friends and family the way you speak to yourself? If it isn't okay to say to someone else, it isn't okay to say to yourself either!

Surround Yourself with Positive People

We surround ourselves with people most like us, so as your confidence grows, your friend group will change.

Jane and Sarah had been friends for nearly a dozen years. Jane's confidence was growing as she grew her business and lived her new life, now free of her ex. When they became friends, Jane and Sarah were very much alike. Two young women with low self-esteem who shared thought processes and even ended up having boys about the same age, then girls.

As Jane's confidence grew, Sarah's stayed the same. Sarah's ex-husband was emotionally and sometimes physically abusive. Hearing terrible things shouted at you over and over for years sinks in and you begin to believe it. As Jane and Sarah's confidence moved upward and downward respectively, they grew apart. Jane developed new friendships with more positive people and Sarah grew more and more bitter and nasty.

You will naturally find yourself less attracted to your negative friends as you build your confidence, but you can get a jump on it and replace them now.

If the negative people in your life are part of your family, limit your exposure to them since you can't really boot people from your family.

Exercise

Exercise is not only good for your body, but it's good for your mind. You develop self-discipline and confidence.

Exercise is also a great way to burn off stress hormones. It gives you purpose and drive and has immeasurable impact on your health. Your heart rate and blood pressure improve. Your weight lowers, which reduces stress on your joints and strain on your circulatory system.

Practice Kindness

When you are kind to others, you feel positive. Simple acts like smiling at a stranger, holding a door open for a mom struggling with a stroller and three kids, or helping an elderly person in the checkout line unload their groceries are all great ways to be kind.

If you want to extend your kindness, make regular donations to a favorite charity, deliver meals to folks who can't make their own or volunteer somewhere. Several times, I've had a person in front of me in a drive-thru line pay for my meal. Pay it forward and pay for the next person's meal.

Being kind to others makes you feel better about yourself. It makes you feel positive, optimistic, and moral.

Simplify Your Life

Identify the essential things in your life. What activities are necessary? Anything not on your list of essential activities moves to the *get rid of it* list. Simplifying your life to include the essentials provides you more time to relax and enjoy.

Simplifying your life also includes your material possessions. I know a woman whose home has every surface decorated with walls full of photos, things she's made and whatever else she can find. Walking into that space is tedious if you're someone who prefers simplification.

Limit yourself to the things you love. Every piece should have value to you. Look at your walls. Do you love what's hanging there? How about your knick-knacks? Do you love the things lying around? Do you use the kitchen appliances you own, or do they sit and gather dust?

Do a true assessment of the people, activities and things in your life and eliminate those which either have no purpose or don't make you happy.

Stop Comparing Yourself to Others

You are a beautiful and unique individual. There is nobody else on earth who is just like you, even if you have a twin sibling. When you compare yourself to others, you're comparing apples to oranges.

You have a set of life experiences that make you the person you are today. You have specific likes and dislikes, career choices, medical histories, and a host of other differences. When you compare yourself to someone else, what you're really doing is validating all the negative things you believe about yourself. She's prettier. Look at her flawless skin. Her hair is so beautiful.

Comparing yourself to someone else steals your joy and makes you feel less than adequate. Embrace who you are and what you've gone through to become this wonderful person. Take pride in the battle scars you have. You survived something to wear those scars. They shouldn't make you feel less worthy, they should make you feel empowered.

Change Your Vocabulary

Words like *should* and *try* need to be removed from your vocabulary. These indicate *some* intention but not enough. Substitute the words *do* and *will.*

- I should try out that new sushi bar downtown sometime
  Replace with: Next week, I will go to the new sushi bar downtown
- I want to try to lose ten pounds
  Replace with: I will lose ten pounds
- I should stop hanging out with Sarah, she's so negative
  Replace with: I will eliminate Sarah from my friend list
- I want to try baking to see if I'm any good at it
  Replace with: I'm going to bake cookies this weekend

Do you see the difference? Don't just think about doing something. Go for it!

I should stop eating ice cream after dinner. Says who? Is this something someone put into your head or do you really want to stop eating ice cream after dinner? Why? Don't allow others to tell you what you should and shouldn't do. You're an adult with a free will to choose your own path. The bigger question is whether eating ice cream after dinner fits into your new life!

Avoid the News

So much of today's news is either negative, depressing or polarized so far to the left or right that there's no way to make sense of it. Watching thirty minutes of news makes you aware of multiple murders, problems of the world, political nonsense and who knows what else.

If you must be up to date on the news, read from a trusted resource online. Pick and choose positive articles and avoid as much negativity as you can.

There's a catch phrase in news reporting, if it bleeds it leads; the gory stories are more popular. It's challenging finding positive news but it's worth it!

Clean Up After Yourself

How depressing is it to walk into your home at the end of a hectic workday and step into a mess? Who wants to spend an entire Saturday picking up?

Develop a habit of picking up after yourself immediately. Do the dishes after the meal, don't leave them for later. Put your dirty clothes in a hamper or basket as soon as you take them off. Have a place for everything and put it there.

If you have a creative hobby, create a place to store it when you aren't working on it. Make your bed every morning as soon as you get up. It promotes better sleep. Put clean clothes away straight out of the dryer. Put groceries away when you get home.

These things must be done at some point, so you may as well do them immediately. Putting them off leads to dreading the task even more than you already do.

Reward Yourself

Develop a system of rewards for yourself. As your habits and positive routines develop, give yourself a reward of some kind. In fact, set up those rewards as you set your goals.

> *I will exercise for 30 minutes, five days this week and my reward will be a new pair of workout pants.*

Make the reward something that motivates and excites you. If it isn't, you won't work toward it.

CHAPTER 21

Breaking Your Routine Will Help You Get Him Back

There is comfort in any routine. You wake up at the same time every day and go through the same morning routine. You know what happens if you skip a step or are forced into a different routine. The whole day feels off and something is forgotten.

You drive the same path to work or school every day. You eat the same things for breakfast and lunch, and you have a work routine you follow.

However, there are a few problems with routines.

A routine doesn't challenge your mind; there is very little opportunity for personal growth. When you change something in your routine, your mind is forced into action. Think about those mornings when you're driving to work and come upon a detour. Suddenly, you're more alert because you just broke your routine and your mind realized you need guidance.

Routines are boring. Where is the fun in life if you live it in the same way, day after day? If you and your ex had a routine life together, one of you probably got bored and that's never a good thing.

Routines make you emotionally cut off. You shift into autopilot and lose touch with yourself and your surroundings. Have you ever found yourself in a daze or just wandering through the day, not really knowing where you are or what you were doing?

If one of your routines is spending your morning train commute reading email on your phone, you miss the opportunity to get to know someone nearby or to observe the scenery on your trip. Your nose is buried in your phone and you're oblivious to the world around you. That mail can wait thirty minutes. Take time to be more curious about your surroundings.

How can changing your routines help you get your ex back?

He knows where you shop for groceries, where you prefer to get your morning coffee and even what flavor you prefer. He knows which brand and flavor of ice cream you buy and what time you go to the gym.

Now that you're apart, you may think he isn't paying attention, but he is. He may try to check on you by passing by where he thinks you might be.

When he goes by the gym and you aren't there at your usual time, he wonders why. If he happens to see you going in before work instead of after, he wonders what caused you to change. Was it that hot guy at the front desk?

If you change where you get your coffee, he wonders who introduced you to this new place and why you now go there.

You're intriguing to him again. Your behaviors don't match what he knows to be the normal activities of your day and he's perplexed. This is a good thing because he's wondering why and whether another man might be the reason.

If you change how you look, you'll really drive him crazy. He wonders what happened to cause you to make such drastic changes. Did you do it for another man? Are you dating or thinking about dating?

These questions plague him and cause him to question the breakup. You are gaining the power position. This is what you want. This is where you want to be. These are the thoughts you want him to have.

So, while breaking your routine is a great thing for you to do for you, it will also have an impact on your ex. He will notice whether directly or indirectly. *He* doesn't see you go to the gym at a new time, but his best friend does. He doesn't see your new hairstyle, but his friend follows you on Instagram and told him all about it.

He will find out.

CHAPTER 22

The How & Why of Self-Care

Self-care is not selfish or self-indulgent. Self-care happens when you take the time to take care of yourself so you can live a life that is healthier, more prosperous, and happier. You have people in your life who rely on you like children or parents, coworkers, employees, or friends. If you don't take care of yourself first, you won't have the tools to take care of others.

Self-care is trending upward, partly because many people feel more anxiety and stress than ever. There are many reasons why our lives in this day and age are more stressful, for example, we put too much pressure on ourselves and spend too many hours on electronics. The news is all negative so if you pay any attention to that, it adds to your stress and anxiety.

Technology speeds up our lives. People expect everything immediately. As I write this now, we're experiencing a global supply chain issue due to COVID-19 and it's forcing everything to slow down. People are so frustrated at a pace that's still faster than what we experienced just fifteen or twenty years ago.

People are lonelier now than before technology took over. You don't need to go visit your friends to chat with them. You can have an ongoing chat throughout the day on your phone and while it's nice to be able to talk to someone all the time, you might miss that face-to-face contact that takes the loneliness out of the day.

There are six types of self-care:

- Physical self-care
- Emotional self-care
- Spiritual self-care
- Social self-care
- Intellectual self-care
- Sensory self-care

Physical Self-Care

This is the most recognized type of self-care. Physical self-care is about taking care of your body, but that doesn't have to be exercise. There are many ways to take care of your body. Make it something you enjoy. If you aren't sure what that is, review these examples:

- Yoga
- Eating healthy meals
- Drinking more water
- Taking a walk
- Zumba
- Running
- Bike riding

Emotional Self-Care

Emotional self-care enables you to get in tune with your emotions. Check in with yourself, uncover what your thought patterns are and become more mindful of triggers. Learn how to work through emotions instead of avoiding or stuffing them down. It's okay to feel sad, hurt, angry, frustrated, and happy. Learn to have more compassion for yourself and your emotions. Some great examples of emotional self-care are:

- Journaling
- Mindfulness and meditation
- Setting boundaries
- Creativity
- A gratitude journal
- Replacing negative self-talk with positive self-talk

Spiritual Self-Care

This can be religion, but it doesn't necessarily need to be. Nourish your spirit and your soul. Develop a connection to something bigger than you and find meaning and purpose for your life. Gain the courage to push through when things get tough. You will inspire hope over and over. A few great ways to practice spiritual self-care are:

- Meditation
- Spending time with nature
- Prayer

- Keeping a gratitude journal
- Donating or volunteering for a charity or a cause you believe strongly in

Intellectual Self-Care

This is the most neglected type of self-care. Intellectual self-care means nurturing and challenging your mind. Determine what your strengths and talents are so you can nurture them further. Develop a new skill, which can help you find a great career. Some great examples of intellectual self-care include:

- Reading a book
- Completing a puzzle
- Learning a new language
- Taking a course on something you're interested in
- Watching documentaries on topics that intrigue you
- Developing new hobbies

Social Self-Care

Humans are social beings, but not everyone is comfortable in social settings. We value connections to other people, even if the circle is small. Social self-care includes having a network of friends and family to lean on during tough times, trust with your deepest secrets and go to when you want to celebrate the victories. Some ways to practice social self-care are:

- Spending time with loved ones

- Having lunch with a friend
- Joining any type of class where you can make new friends who share your interests
- Reconnecting with an old friend
- Speaking to a stranger while you're waiting in line

Sensory Self-Care

Tweaking your senses is a very effective way to become mindful. Some examples of sensory self-care include burning a scented candle, taking a warm bath, spending time in nature, listening to music you enjoy and walking barefoot in the grass.

CHAPTER 23

Your Vision for Your Life

Everyone has core beliefs which focus on several areas of life such as power, love, sex, friendship, spirituality, men, and so on. You probably have a reality you cling to based on your beliefs and experiences. Some realities are formed based on what you think you should do, rather than on what you want to do.

You have a job you hate because you should pay the bills. Of course, you should pay the bills, but what if you loved your job, even at the expense of part of your salary? Would you do it? If it meant being happy, would you at least consider it?

Sadly, some shake their heads no at these questions. I'm fortunate because I love what I do. I wake up excited and ready face the day.

Do you know what you want? Have you ever thought about what you want? Have you ever spent even a few moments dreaming of the life you could have if there were no roadblocks?

A Funny Thing Happened on the Way to My Dream

I dare you to live a life of mediocrity! I challenge you to remain stagnant.

See how ridiculous it sounds?

You can do better. You can be a better mother, girlfriend, friend, daughter, boss, and coworker. What will it take to make positive changes? It will take trying things you've never tried before and failing more times than you want to.

If you allow yourself to do these things, you will have many new and fun experiences. You will embrace failure and recognize it as an opportunity to grow and learn. You will meet new friends and build your confidence.

A funny thing happens on the way to realizing your dreams. You develop self-worth, higher self-esteem, and greater confidence. You reach your goals and achieve dreams. You believe in yourself, and you know you can.

Continue through these five steps to change your attitude and perception of what you think you know. Allow time in your life to become an adventurer.

Explore what you think is true about yourself. Expand your horizons. Unveil the adventurer who lies within. Allow her to shine and explode your life into something truly wonderful!

Time to Recognize Limiting Beliefs

Why do you think you either don't know what you want out of your life or haven't yet pursued your dreams? It's not because you aren't capable. Don't tell me that because I won't believe it, not even for a moment! I've got a better answer!

Your Limiting Beliefs Are Holding You Back!

Let's look at a limiting belief. I like to use power. Like me, you hold some belief about power. Perhaps you believe that power is indicative of meanness because someone who held power over you in your past was also mean.

If you seek to become a powerful person, maybe a leader, this belief will keep you from your dream. Let's look at how the thought process goes.

> I want to be powerful ⇨ Powerful people are mean ⇨
> I don't want to be mean ⇨ I can't be powerful.

This is a simplistic way of looking at it, but this is an example of a self-limiting belief. You have created a reality based on a flawed belief. Do you know any powerful people who are not mean? I'm sure you do. Think of a teacher you favored or a boss you thought was great. Those were people with power over you, and they debunk your belief.

Find your limiting beliefs by examining your dreams and determining which you feel are most unattainable. Even if you're practicing positive self-talk, limiting beliefs can lurk beneath the surface.

Let's look at an example.

Suppose you're worried about money. How does this stress make you feel? Probably anxious, maybe angry because you feel like you can't catch a break. You might feel hopeless that your situation will never get any better.

Now, sit with some of those feelings. If you feel anxious about not having enough money, what's the real pressure point? *"What will my family think if I can't make it on my own?"* or, *"If I can't live in this expensive neighborhood, people will think less of me."*

Your limiting beliefs in this example might be focused on people thinking less of you because you're struggling financially. Maybe if you're angry, you're thinking something like, *"Life isn't fair."* Hopelessness might go something like, *"I will never be able to get my head above water—I'm not smart enough to figure it out."*

Getting Rid of Limiting Beliefs

Once you identify limiting beliefs, it's time to get rid of them.

Take one limiting belief and write it on a piece of paper. Sit and look at it. How does it make you feel? Angry? Sad?

Anxious? Fearful? How strong are these feelings? Write this down with your belief.

> *I can't make enough money. I get strong feelings of fear and anxiety when I read this statement.*

Now, face the truth versus the belief.

Perhaps you believe you can't make enough money because you aren't smart enough, you didn't go to college, or someone has told you this in the past.

Is this true? There are many people who have made more than enough money without a college education. In fact, it's often true that blue collar jobs pay better, especially when you're younger. There is rarely a true dead-end job, and many places of employment will help you pay for the added education you need to advance.

I know it's hard to change this belief, but to change your course, you must change your belief.

Next, replace this limiting belief with a better one. For example, *"I can make enough money if I find a second job."* Or *"I can have enough money if I cut back on my expenses."* Even better is, *"My financial problems of the past have taught me some valuable lessons and I am prepared to put those lessons to use now."*

Your last step is to look at your new statement. How does it make you feel? Energized? Hopeful? Excited? Motivated? I bet it does. Before you can solve the issue, be it happiness or your finances, you must turn your negative thought patterns into positive ones.

Your Beliefs About Being Single

It's time for some fun! Think about your beliefs regarding your last relationship, or past relationships in general. Write them down.

Here are a few examples:

- I can't trust my ex
- Only lucky people find true love
- To get my ex back, I will have to sacrifice
- I'm too _____ for him to come back to me
- The problem with relationships is that all guys ______
- I'll never get over him

Live the Part

Once you see your limiting beliefs, replace them, and start living the part!

Believing this new statement is irrelevant at this point. Force your mind to latch onto something new. The best way to do that is to act like it's already true.

If your limiting belief was that you're too fat for anyone to love you, you need to act like the thinner version of yourself you dream of. Where does she go? What does she do during the day? How does she eat? Who are her friends? What does her wardrobe look like? Does she hang out at the pool in a swimsuit?

Some of these actions will take true courage on your part. It is facing that fear of jumping out of an airplane that helps you overcome it. It's wearing that swimsuit at the pool, not caring what others think, that gives you the courage and gumption to try something bolder!

Obviously, you need to be reasonable. If your limiting belief is financial and your new belief is having the money to do what you want, you can't just go willy-nilly and spend money you don't have, but you could build a vision board representative of things you want to have, do, or be when your finances are in order.

One More Thing

You've created a life centered around your limiting beliefs. Depending on how old you are, these beliefs may reach back decades. You build the life you have based on what you believe.

If you believe you're not good enough, you won't be motivated to try. You'll be labeled as an underachiever. You might work a job well below your true potential. You may not manage your finances because you've already decided you'll live a life of paycheck-to-paycheck stress. You probably won't have many friends or be motivated to go out and meet new people. Your lifestyle validates your beliefs, and you even say things like, *"See! I've been stuck in this entry-level job for ten years! I told you I wasn't good enough!"*

Turning your entire lifestyle around is something I know you can do! I believe in you! It will be scary! I am not going to lie to you. There may be days you wake up scared to death at the plan you made, but you must push yourself forward. Face those fears and be brave enough to make the changes I know you're capable of.

My mom is befuddled by me. I never read. In fact, the last book I read was Charlotte's Web in 4th grade! I'm kidding, but that's not far from the truth. My three older sisters read everything. My mom can't believe that I became the writer in the family.

Did I have limiting beliefs? I sure did. But I overcame them. I threw them out the window because they were hurting me. I write because I decided I could, and I like it. Am I smarter than you? I highly doubt it. **I know you can overcome your self-limiting beliefs, too**!

Do you see the power you gain when you throw those beliefs away?

If you're stuck in an entry-level job, go back to school or seek training to move up. Apply for a promotion or change companies. You don't need to live paycheck to paycheck. Get a second job or cut back on your expenses. There are always things you can do to make positive changes. Set your mind to doing them and kill off those limiting beliefs.

These changes won't happen overnight and simply saying to yourself, "I am thin" doesn't make you so. Regardless of the belief you need to turn around, there is hard work to be done, but the payoff is so enormous that it's well worth the effort!

CHAPTER 24

What is Your Story?

Every day, you add to your story. Your story is the events of your life up until now that have shaped the person you are today. You might not like the story so far, but there is still a whole lifetime worth of story to be written - and you are the author!

What's the Big Deal About Having a Story?

Your story makes you interesting. It gives you something to share with people you talk to. Not that you share the entire story, but something that applies to the situation you're in at that moment. For example, if you've decided to coach your son's soccer team, your story for the other team parents might be how you played soccer as a kid. For the organization asking you to be the coach, your story might also include any experience you have in managing people or working with kids.

When you date, your story keeps a guy intrigued. You share snippets of it with him from time to time, never giving the entire story away at once, and he becomes more interested in you.

Up until now, you probably haven't paid much attention to what you add to your story, but I encourage you to be more mindful of what's included in your story.

How do You Write a Great Story?

Take Risks

Do things that feel risky. Do something that scares you like riding a roller coaster or going out to dinner by yourself.

Face fears. The risk is in the unknown. This is something that scares you for some reason and experiencing it is risky in your own mind. You might be afraid of heights, so a risk would be sitting at the top of the bleachers at a sports event or walking close to the railing at a multi-story mall.

The great thing about taking a risk, facing a fear, is that when you've finished, you feel exhilarated. Your confidence grows with each fear you conquer. And it doesn't matter how scared you were or whether you fully went through with it or not. Maybe you only made it to row five of the bleachers. That's a start and you should be proud if it!

Experience Life

It's easy to sit on the sidelines and watch others experience life, but what if you experience it yourself? Instead of reading about the beautiful tulips in Holland, go visit. Instead of imagining dragging your toes through the sand on the beach, find a beach and do it. Don't just dream of doing things. Get out there and do them.

These experiences add great chapters to your story, chapters that belong just to you. If you want to learn how to draw, take art lessons. If you want to learn to ride a horse, go learn it. Whatever it is you want to try, go for it. Don't just sit and watch someone else do it on a YouTube video. Get out there and do it.

Get Passionate

What lights you up? What gets you so excited when you see it or read about it? Is it animal welfare? Is it helping the needy? Is it volunteering at nursing homes to spend time with people who don't have any visitors? Is it politics? Is it being a hospital volunteer? What is it?

Find something about which you are passionate and pursue it. Get involved. Work on Special Olympics events. Sit at pet adoption tables during special events. Get a few friends to go with you to the nursing home so more people can enjoy visitors.

Passions drive you to do things for others which makes you feel great about yourself, as well as doing something great for someone else.

Get a Hobby

Having a hobby keeps you busy. It helps you develop new skills and provides you with an opportunity to teach those skills to someone else.

Hobbies are a wonderful way to fill your time, especially now when you need a mental distraction. They range from starting a foodie blog to building furniture and everything in between.

The best part about hobbies is that sometimes you can share them with your partner. This is a win-win. You both get to do something you enjoy, and you can do it together. Combine hobbies, like your love of photography with his love of antique cars. Go to shows and photograph the cars or photograph him working on an antique care.

A Challenge

I challenge you to start writing your future story today. Make a list of things you can do to make your story more interesting. This type of story will help you build your confidence in ways you never imagined. Each risk you take, each fear you face, each thing you become passionate about, and each hobby builds your confidence a little more.

But don't just sit there and stare at that list. Go do the things on the list! It's no good if you don't get out there and get started!

CHAPTER 25

The Days of Living in the Past are Over, Starting Today

It's easy to get stuck in the past, whether it's the recent past or the distant past. People do this when there are unresolved issues that keep them stuck there. Chances are, you've been avoiding facing these issues head-on because there is pain associated with the memories.

But here's the thing. If you don't bring it up and unpack it, it won't go away. It's there, festering like wound that won't heal. The only way to allow it to heal is to feel the pain and give it some air. In time, it won't hurt so much.

Depending on your pain, you might require professional intervention. This is okay. It's not shameful to seek help, it shows you're aware of your mind and body and that your issues are deeper than a book like this can fix.

Examine Your Life

Dig into what those issues are. What is holding you back or keeping you stuck? Journaling can help you discover what's lurking, but sometimes you know the solution and find it in your own words. Use your journal to make a list of your past experiences, mistakes and problematic moments that bother you.

Writing things down often relieves your mind of the burden and frees up space for the present. It provides more room to sort through these past issues and find meaningful solutions.

At the end of each week, go back through that week's entries and see if anything kept appearing. Was there a particular person or event that really bothered you? Dig into why.

Look for the Lessons

Many hurtful experiences of your past contain lessons, but you get so wrapped up in the shame or pain that you miss the lessons.

This breakup was painful but in the last step, you learned some things you may have done to contribute. If any of them applied to you, there are lessons there for you to extract. Many of them are low confidence moves, so continuing through Step Three is the best way forward, but when you look at each mistake, what is the individual lesson to be learned?

In every mistake, there is a lesson, but the challenge is to move beyond feeling badly about the mistake so you can see the lesson. Most lessons are right there in front of you, but you choose not to see them, or you can't see them because of the pain or embarrassment.

Remember, you're a human being, not made to be perfect. Cut yourself some slack.

Forgive

Are you sensing that some of these things come up repeatedly? Forgiveness is one, but that's because it's so powerful. Forgiving isn't a sign of weakness. It's a sign of strength.

When you consider something that needs to be forgiven, ask yourself whether the person who hurt you intended to do so. Sometimes, people do things because they feel it's for your benefit. Other times, they just plain didn't think about the consequences of their actions.

Their reasons aside, forgiving is letting go of the past. It isn't for the person you're forgiving. It's for you.

Along with forgiving, stop waiting for an apology that may never come. People put so much weight on apologies, but the truth is that they don't fix anything and waiting for one is just a nifty way to keep living in the past.

If you struggle to forgive, write a letter to the person you need to forgive and lay it all out on a piece of paper. Vent and get rid of whatever you're carrying. Then burn it, shred it, or do whatever you need to do to destroy it. You should feel better for getting it off your chest.

End the Victim Mentality

There is a payoff for being a victim, but that doesn't mean it's good for you.

The problem with being the victim and never accepting responsibility for your life is that you don't learn from your mistakes. When you blame someone else, you're giving them power in your life. Take back that power by accepting responsibility.

Practice Mindfulness

Mindfulness is being present in the here and now, so if you're being mindful, you aren't living in the past.

When you catch yourself focusing on something from the past, refocus your energy on right now. What do you see, smell, hear, feel and taste?

Grow Your Circle

You may have a circle of friends, but you can always add more. As you explore new passions, you will find new friends. As you develop hobbies, you will find new friends there too. Changing careers may inject new friends into your life.

You can never have a support system that's too large. Surround yourself with positive people who share your interests and will have your back. When you have fun things to look forward to, you spend less time looking back.

Always Work on That Vision

A great way to stop living in the past is to work on the things in your future vision. Work on the version of you that you envision.

Have goals and spend time working toward them. When you're working toward things you want in the future or a future version of yourself, you aren't spending time in the past.

Conquer Your Addictions

When most people see the word addiction, their mind immediately goes to drugs and alcohol, but with today's technology, there are many others like:

- Social media
- Video games
- Gambling
- Gossip
- Fast food
- Sugar
- Soda
- Binge watching TV
- Anything you can't live without that is taking time and energy away from realizing your vision

Addictions steal your time and energy. Worrying about how many likes you got for your latest Instagram post is fruitless and it's a low confidence move. If your only reason for being on social media is to see how many people *like* your stuff, you need a social media detox.

Look internally instead of externally for approval. Do all those likes advance you toward your vision? Does spending all that time posting about what you ate for lunch and how great you look in your new outfit move you closer to your goals?

Your addiction is holding you back and keeping you from the life you want to live. Wean yourself off whatever it is and start seeing positive changes!

Stop Waiting for "Normal"

If you wait for things to return to normal before you do something, you'll be waiting a long time. The COVID pandemic is a great example of stalling people's lives. *I'll start my new business when things get back to normal.* What is normal? Maybe we will never return to what pre-COVID life. You'll wait forever.

This is a stall tactic, plain and simple. It's your fear talking. If you can place a parameter on doing something, like *when normal returns*, you will never do it. Change is an ongoing thing. What was normal a week ago may not be normal today. Instead of pinning your future on waiting for normal, just go for it!

Be a Little Better Every Day

Wake up each day with the determination that you will do something to improve yourself. Maybe you work out a little harder at the gym or you sign up for a class on a new hobby you want to try. Decide to avoid sugar for a few hours or go up that set of bleachers all the way to the top.

Stay focused on now, not yesterday. Don't worry about what happened yesterday or even last week because you can't change it anyway. Focus on being a better version of yourself today and then wake up and do the same tomorrow!

And Finally, Let Go of Toxic People

Toxic people in your life are dragging you down. They are full of negativity, and they represent the old you, the you that you're trying to improve.

Toxic people live in the past, they aren't forgivers or risk-takers, and they like to play the victim role. You're already letting go of those negative behaviors and picking up on the positive ones they're trying to avoid. It's impossible to move forward with toxic friendships.

It's not fun to cut people out of your life, but this is for you, not them. Maybe they'll see the new you and decide to join your journey. Great! Let them in, but if they're faking it, they must go.

CHAPTER 26

Are You a Student or a Victim?

After experiencing a negative life event like a breakup, it's easy to settle into a victim mentality. Suddenly, nothing goes as it should. Your boyfriend broke up with you, you dropped your phone in the toilet, your car died, and the cat is shaking his head as if even he can't believe how bad it is.

I can see how you might feel like a victim, but what good is it doing? I propose that you become a student. Compare to see how they're different.

A Victim Sheds Responsibility but a Student Accepts and Corrects

As a victim, you accept no responsibility for anything that happens in your life. It's not your fault the electricity got shut off. Stupid electric company rips people off. It's not your fault you got a D on the last test; the teacher is a jerk.

With a student mentality, you say, *"Well I forgot to pay the electric bill, but next month, I'll put a reminder on my phone, so I pay it a few days ahead of time!"* You learn from the mistake, and you move forward.

When you don't accept responsibility for events in your life, you can't improve your situation. Since it's not your doing, you can't undo it either.

A Victim Eagerly Tells a Tragic Story While a Student Builds an Interesting One

As a victim, you want everyone to your tragic story so they can lavish pity on you. *"Oh, you poor thing! Life is just beating you up!"* This attention makes you feel special, important, noticed.

Meanwhile, the student is out bungee jumping, visiting the nursing home with a therapy pet, not worried about what others think.

A bonus of the victim mentality is attention. People feel sorry for you. They want to do things to help you, perhaps even give you money.

After a few incidents of this, these same people will avoid you because you're a Debbie Downer and nobody wants to hang out with her too long.

A Victim Thrives on Drama While a Student Finds Other Means of Entertainment

Most men hate drama. Let me rephrase – confident, high-quality men hate drama because it's usually due to some sort of problem being blown out of proportion, or a one hundredth retelling of a terrible thing that happened to someone.

A student is trying new things, exploring her world, and looking for new ways to grow and learn. She watches the sunset over the water and shares an ice cream cone with her dog, Butch.

Boredom causes you to do things you probably shouldn't do, like dig into someone's drama, or blow up your own situation into a drama. If you're busy facing your fears, taking risks, doing things for others, and exploring all life has to offer, you don't have time for drama.

A man would much rather hear about your white-water rafting trip than how your best friend's boyfriend dumped her for the tenth time.

A Victim Is Pessimistic While a Student Is Eager to Learn More

This makes me think of the favorite Winnie the Pooh character, Eeyore. This lovable gray creature slogs through the Hundred-Acre Woods with his ears down and his spirits even lower. He makes us smile because he's cute in his own way, but in real life, this type of *"everything is always wrong"* or *"everything bad always happens to me"* attitude gets old fast.

Spending all your time in an inquiring mindset doesn't leave much time for wallowing. You're too busy trying a new cooking class, learning a new hobby, or challenging someone to a cut-throat tennis match.

Seeing the downside of life puts you in a brutal depression. While it feels comforting to have people constantly saying, *"Oh no, everything will turn around soon, don't you worry"* or *"Don't worry honey, we're all here for you,"* people don't want to spend all their time propping you up when they can be doing something fun and engaging.

A Victim Feels Attacked While a Student Grows

You just turned a big report in to your boss. You wait and wait, and he comes back and says, *"This is great, but do you think you can add more to this section on...?"*

The victim feels completely defeated and attacked. You busted your butt on that report and all he can do is pick away at one little missing piece. What the heck!?! That's the last time you'll pull an all-nighter to get *his* work done!

The student says, *"Sure! Was there anything else you thought could be changed or added? I'd be happy to get right on this for you!"* The student sees the opportunity to learn and looks great in front of her boss because she shows eagerness to improve.

Constructive criticism is a part of life. If delivered properly, it's intended to help you, not attack you or hurt your feelings.

The Friends of Victims Are Victims While the Friends of Students Are Adventurers!

Victims attract other victims . People love to wallow together, while people who aren't carrying around a victim mentality will quickly shy away from the wallowers because it bogs them down. If your friends are wallowing in self-pity, chances are you are doing the same.

Students hang out with people who see life as an adventure. Students want to grow and do new things. Sure, they'll slip into moments of frustration – nobody is perfect – but they shrug off this type of thing by getting out there and doing something.

Confident, high-quality men do not want to hang out with someone who is a downer, wallowing in self-pity, or always seeing the dark side of things. They'll scoot out of your life faster than you can say ala-kazaam.

How to End the Victim Mentality

There is good news. If you feel one or more of these victim descriptors fits you, there is hope! Here are the steps.

Change Your Language

Instead of saying, *"You make me so angry"* or *"They are always picking on me,"* try something like, *"It makes me feel angry when you speak to me that way"* or *"I don't like it when the whole family picks on my flaws."*

In this language reset, you accept responsibility for what's happening. You own your reaction, and don't imply someone else forced you to respond in a specific way. It's a subtle nuance, but it makes a big difference!

Stop Fighting Life

When you are a victim, you fight the current. Rather than accepting what comes your way, and adapting or repairing what's broken, you buck the system. Victims feel helpless to make any changes in their lives.

You are in control, and you are not helpless. People don't pull themselves out of misery because they're comfortable there. The emotions are familiar. There is a payoff.

When you take control of your life and roll with what comes, you feel empowered. You stop waiting for the next bad thing to come along.

Treat Yourself Like You'd Treat Others

We treat ourselves worse than we would ever treat someone else. The things you say to and about yourself in your head or aloud never cross your lips about another person.

Self-loathing is a result of years and years spent being a victim. Take time to dig into old wounds and core beliefs. What is compounding your victim identity? How did you get here to begin with?

Practice positive self-talk. Stop putting yourself down with things like, *"You're worthless"* or *"Nobody could ever love you."* Take time to see a therapist to work through those old wounds if necessary. It is difficult to sort through them on your own.

Dismantle Faulty Beliefs

You probably think you know what you believe. In a past chapter, you examined limiting beliefs. A great example is this one, *"I want to make a lot of money."* What happens if you dig into your beliefs about money?

You believe you want to make a lot of money, but you also believe any or all of these:

- People with a lot of money are jerks – "Those Lexus drivers will run you down – jerks!"
- Money is hard to make and harder to keep
- Money can't buy happiness
- Rich people use their money to control the lives of others
- I'd have to win the lottery to get rich

While you think you believe you want to make a lot of money, these beliefs are roadblocks, because, at your core, you think having a lot of money is bad in some way.

Dismantle some of your beliefs and see what truly lies at the root. Do you have beliefs that are opposite to one another?

Practice Gratitude

Challenge yourself for ten days to find five new things each day for which you can be grateful.

Get a journal and write at least five new things every day. When you see the good in your life, it's harder to find the bad. You realize life isn't quite as bad as you thought it was after all, and things become a little brighter.

Develop Positive Affirmations

In the victim mentality, there is very little positive running through your head. To change this, notice those negative thoughts as they chug by, and come up with positive counterparts.

Negative thoughts are housed way down in your unconscious, and they are difficult to uproot unless you change them into positive thoughts and keep repeating the positives.

Be sure to include thoughts like, *"I am responsible for my own life"* and, *"I can do anything I set my mind to."*

Do Something for Someone Else

I can remember watching some show on cable a few years ago on this man whose skin was like tree bark. It is some rare skin disorder, and this man was in tremendous pain. His body was becoming more and more deformed by his condition every day.

After watching how hard he fought and how he endured so much pain every day, just to get through life, I said to myself, *"My life is great!"*

There are people who are truly suffering from disease or misfortune. They are victims of fires, floods, or other natural disasters like tornadoes and hurricanes; people with debilitating diseases or those who are enduring cancer; elderly people who sometimes have no family to come and visit with them.

Find a way to help someone else. Shovel an elderly neighbor's driveway. Take a bowl of soup or some packages of herbal tea to a neighbor suffering from cancer. Find a nursing home or rehabilitation center near you and just go visit.

When you're helping someone else, you forget your own problems. Be the uplifting force in another person's life and recognize you can feel good in a way that doesn't involve making people feel sorry for you.

Break the Pattern

To find a great guy or get your ex back, you must **become a student of life**. Embrace what life throws at you by tossing your hair back and laughing at it. Learn the lesson and apply it moving forward.

Become an adventurer. Be grateful for what you do have in your life and recognize that you have much to offer someone else.

Turn that negative language you're using on yourself into positive affirmations. You are a great individual, and some guy would be lucky to have you – once you drop the victim stuff!

CHAPTER 27

It's Time to Date (Other Men)

Before you turn to the next chapter, stick around and read this. There are several good reasons for dating other men, not the least of which is to prove to your ex that if he can date other women, you can date other men. But there are other benefits.

You Can Compare

I don't know your dating history. Your ex might be your first love or your fifth. It doesn't matter. Regardless, date multiple men at a time so you can compare.

Date different types of men. Find guys who aren't like the men you've dated in the past. Then go back and assess the date. What did you like? What did you dislike?

You may surprise yourself and find that while you always shunned the biker dude, he turns out to be a super nice guy who is sensitive and intelligent.

Build a list of the qualities you want and don't want in a man based on this new information.

You Gain New Friends

Even if you go out with a guy and decide you don't want to date him, you can still make a friend. One date is not a marriage proposal. It's a chance to get to know someone a little better. Two dates mean you learn a little more. And it goes on from there.

You can never have enough friends and having a guy friend can be helpful when you're trying to interpret the behavior of other men. What you need to be careful of is that he doesn't have stronger feelings for you than you do for him. Be honest about wanting a friendship only. Otherwise, if he has strong feelings for you, he'll feel hurt when you talk about other men.

You Gain the Notice of Your Ex

Your ex is watching, whether directly or through mutual friends. When he broke up with you, he expected you to wallow and sit at home brooding while he went out and dated other women. You are his Plan B. If he doesn't find anything better, he will crawl back to you, and you'll be there waiting.

Well, wait a minute. What just happened? You went out on a date? No, not one date, multiple dates? What the heck is going on? You're not wallowing, and you look great. You got your hair cut and the color is awesome. You've been working out and oh man, he wishes he'd made a different choice now!

CHAPTER 28

Are You Ready For Step 4?

By now, you are feeling more confident. It won't all come at once. But if you continue to do the things in Step Three, your confidence will grow. There is never a time in your life when you should stop trying to grow and build yourself. Life events will always be there to take you down a peg or two so building up is a continuous effort.

Step Four is a big one and it's time to decide if you still want your ex back. Many women reach the end of Step Three and decide their ex is no longer worthy of them. They move on and find a new guy.

Still other women want their ex back, and that's why you're here. You're making this decision with more knowledge and confidence than you started with. You better understand his motivation and what he's thinking. You've assessed whether he's capable of love and mentally healthy enough. You've spent plenty of time building your own confidence.

Step Four assumes you still want to get your ex back. If, however, you've decided not to, I encourage you to visit my other website, **WhoHoldstheCardsNow.com** and read the section about **finding a guy** (www.whoholdsthecardsnow.com/i-want-to-find-a-guy/). I also encourage you to read more on understanding men.

You are ready to move on to Step Four if:

- You have reined in your emotions
- You have fully assessed the breakup
- You have become an independent woman, ready for an interdependent relationship
- You have made positive changes in your life
- You've broken your routine
- You've implemented a self-care plan and are practicing self-care regularly
- You have a vision for your life
- You're writing your story
- You've stopped living in the past
- You are a student, not a victim
- You have dated at least three other men since your breakup

step 4

Time to Toy with His Psyche

Sometimes, I get a little blow-back on this step, but this is exactly what you're about to do. Remember reading that he needs to overcome the negative feelings he has about you and your relationship?

While you've been taking care of yourself and rebuilding your confidence, you've also been giving him time to do that.

It's time to tweak his good memories of your relationship so he can replace negatives with positives. If you recall, one of the deal breakers is not having enough history together and this is why. He needs positive memories of the two of you together to replace negative memories.

You can't create positive memories now and expect those to replace the negative memories.

How do we tweak his memories and tap into those positives?

You use *slip in and slip out.* This is fun and will tweak those good memories. Soon, you'll show off the new you and the new life you've built using social media. Even if you blocked him or he blocked you, he'll find out. He has feelers out there.

At this stage, you want him to think a few things:

- He is potentially losing you and if you recall, guys don't like to lose their stuff
- You're a new version of yourself, confident, happy, and dating a little
- What's good for the goose is good for the gander, or in this case, what's good for the gander is good for the goose – he wants to be able to have you on the hook while he dates other women; you're going to remind him that you can date other guys

I know these actions are counter-intuitive, but they will work! By this time, he's ready to replace negative memories and emotions with positive. By writing him the letter and using slip in/ slip out, you deliver those positive memories and emotions.

You're showing him you aren't sitting in a dark room, pining away for him like he thinks you are. He'll be surprised and somewhat intrigued because you haven't acted as he thought you would. It's that old mystery and challenge thing again!

You aren't angry texting him. You aren't calling him begging him to come back. You worked on yourself and now you're enjoying the fruits of your labor.

Your behavior is mysterious, and he feels challenged to present the best version of *himself*, if he wants to win you back. He is operating under the idea that you're at his beck and call. When he's done sowing his wild oats, you'll be waiting in the wings, ready to beg him back.

He sees you aren't pining away. You aren't on his hook. Just like him, you're out there dating other guys. If he can do it, **so can you**!

CHAPTER 29

The Slip In/Slip Out Method

Will no contact make him move on or reconsider? Does the power of silence after a breakup draw him back to you? The conventional no contact rule has been tossed around a lot and it's time to toss it out!

Instead, here is a combination of contact and no contact. Before you get excited and run off and text him, learn how it works.

If you totally go no contact, you may be out of sight, out of mind. If you're out of his thoughts for too long, he will forget about you. Here's a better idea.

It's called Slip In/Slip Out.

You slip into his life with a statement or question that confirms it's over and then slip out by breaking contact again.

This is bold and confident and sends a message that you are moving on and growing stronger. More importantly, you aren't sitting around waiting for him, like he thinks you are.

Here's how slip in/slip out works. You send him a text that reads something like this:

- "Hey, can you throw my red sweater in a box and leave it outside your door?"
- "Quick question, what was the name of the guy who gave you boxing lessons?"
- "We're headed to Aruba. What was the name of that great bar on the water?"

These texts make him squirm, leaving him to think:

- "Wow, she wants the rest of her stuff…it must really be over"
- "Shit, if she takes boxing lessons, she will meet that guy Jeff who wants her bad"
- "Aruba? Who the f*** is she going to Aruba with? We just broke up!"

These are *exactly* the thoughts you want him to have. You're toying with his psyche. He's questioning all his actions. You're reminding him of **your relationship** just in case you had disappeared from his thoughts.

There are a couple things to remember:

- This is a powerful tactic so don't overdo it; once may be enough
- You're role reversing by delivering what looks like the final break up
- Don't have a weak moment and spill your guts to try to get him back; it will set you back
- He needs to come back on his own time
- Be sure to follow through and pick up your sweater, take the boxing lessons or go to Aruba
- Act casual, it confuses him more

You are saying you're ready to move on. He can't believe you're taking such bold actions so soon. He still thinks he can come back to you at any moment, and you will be sitting there waiting for him.

And then you go silent again? He's asking himself, *"What gives?"*

He thinks that because he dumped you, you are grieving and at his beck and call. He imagines you're curled up in the fetal position somewhere with ice cream stuck to your chin, your hair a mess and red eyes from the crying.

Now he knows you're not doing any of those things!

When you send your goodbye letter, slip in/slip out with statements confirming it's over, and go silent again, you turn the breakup on its head and confuse your ex.

Are you bluffing? Yes, because you have nothing to lose. You are already broken up. He has no idea what you will do next, and he's desperate to find out!

This is a good thing.

His mind shifts. He realizes you are not his backup plan. Guys break up to test the waters. But what many of them don't realize is that the waters aren't always better, in fact the waters usually suck.

Now that he knows you're growing stronger and potentially moving on, he can't treat his new single's life with the same vigor and excitement he once had. Door number two is closing fast, and that door is you. He questions the breakup and thinks about the great memories you had.

And memories are tough to manage!

If your relationship has enough memories prior to the break, he will have a weak moment and you need to be ready for it.

You are toying with the male psyche and providing yourself with the best odds of stirring his emotions and getting him to capitulate. You are doing the exact opposite of what you want to do and what he thinks you will do.

And you're doing it all with confidence. Stay upbeat with your slip in/slip out messages and don't act angry. Be happy! If you can't, delay until you can.

You have opened the lines of communication and he can reconsider. The combination of the letter and slip in/slip out has him thinking about you, but not just about you.

> *He is now recalling positive memories and they're starting to take the place of the negatives he was recalling before.*

This method of the no contact rule works because you only practice radio silence for short periods of time before reaching out in a way that leaves him wondering what the heck is going on.

BOOM!

CHAPTER 30

What's Good for the Goose Is Good for the Gander, or Vice Versa

Your ex is dating. This isn't news to you, and you already know why he's dating. At the end of Step Three, your instructions were to date other men. What's good for the gander is good for the goose. One of his thoughts when he broke up with you was that he would date other women to see if he could find someone that he liked better than you.

However, what he never envisioned was you dating other men. He is operating on the idea that whenever he decides to take you back, not only will you be waiting breathlessly for him, but you will be just as he left you. Single.

But now he sees that you're dating, and not only are you dating, but you look and act different. This is alarming. You aren't acting as he expected, and he doesn't quite know what to do with this information.

This is where things get really interesting.

He sees you having fun and dating other men and it messes with his head. This wasn't part of the story he wrote about the breakup. He writes a glorious movie with a plot that included coming back to you when he was good and ready. His dream plot is now becoming his nightmare movie! You aren't waiting in the wings, teary-eyed and waiting for him to return.

You're moving on and up.

Doing these things will scare you and they're not at all what you expected to read, but that's the point isn't it? That's why you're reading this book. You're learning to reprogram your mind, in part, to think more like a guy so you can relate to him and understand what he's doing and thinking.

If you cheated a little and moved on to this step before you dated other men, I encourage you to do that now. Get on Match.com or another dating app and find yourself three or four guys who interest you.

Shoot them a wink or a thumbs up or whatever and see what happens. If your friends can set you up with a great guy, let them. Remember, dating isn't a marriage proposal. It's going out with someone to learn more about them. That's it. Go on fun dates, like bowling, hiking or other fun activities. Dates don't need to be dinner and sex!

He's having fun and dating other women. For now, you've lost him, but by dating and having fun yourself, you lessen how much fun he is having, and you put him in a position of worrying that he might not have you to come back to when he's done sowing his wild oats.

That's exactly where you want him to be!

CHAPTER 31

Mystery – What Is It and How Do You Create It?

Men find you mysterious at first, but once you've told your entire story, the mystery fades unless you work to keep it alive.

But what is mystery? Mystery happens when:

- You take risks
- You don't share your entire story and keep some things to yourself
- You keep him guessing
- You break your routine
- You give him space

A guy wants you to do these things. He's rooting for you!

When you first date, he knows little about you. You're mysterious. It's like opening one of those gifts that's been wrapped inside another gift five or six times. Every layer opens to reveal a new gift.

Men love to unwrap the mystery, which is why it's so important to tell your story in bits and pieces instead of all at once. Once the entire story is told, find new ways to be mysterious by continuing to grow chase new hobbies and experiences!

He will eventually learn your whole story, but that should be a long time from now. Don't keep important things from him like that you have children or can't have children if the conversation gets to that point. The bits and pieces you hold back are tidbits of your story, like how you and a friend decided to take a road trip to Vegas after you graduated from college or how you got started making candles for a hobby.

Don't change who you are or lie, just be mysterious. Try some of these suggestions.

Break His Label

You might see a new neighbor wearing a plaid shirt, socks pulled to his knees with loafers and geeky glasses and decide he's a geek. Then, you see him in another setting and almost don't recognize him because he's wearing tight jeans with a Henley and tennis shoes. The geek turned into a hottie!

When a man first sees you, whether he realizes it or not, he places a label on you. If your hair was pulled up into a tight bun and you just came from the office, he might label you one way, but then you let your hair down, take your jacket off and loosen up a little, he sees someone different. Now, he's intrigued because you broke free of the label that he assigned you.

You're already breaking the label your ex put on you with the many changes you've made, but if you get back together, you need to continue to make small changes to keep him on his toes. These can be anything from changing the flavor of coffee you order to getting a complete makeover.

Give Him Space

There are a couple of reasons to give a guy his space. Many men are not equipped to manage their emotions, so when they experience something that's emotionally difficult, they need some space to sort through those emotions.

The second reason is to allow him space to hang out with his friends, whether that's a physical space like a man cave, or it's just allowing him to spend time with his friends without being penalized.

Let him spend time on his hobby while you spend time on yours. If he wants to hang out with his friends, hang out with yours and if he's going through something heavy, let him come to you when he's ready to talk. Don't keep bugging him to share it with you. He will when he's ready.

And, of course, there are the ways to create mystery we've already discussed:

- Take some risks
- Break your routine
- Don't tell him your whole story at once

CHAPTER 32

What Is Challenge and How Do You Challenge Him?

Challenge and mystery are often lumped together because they're two key things you can do in your relationship to keep a guy on his toes. The goal is to stay one step ahead of him.

If he's planning to go to the gym, you've already gone. If he's getting ready for work, you've got his clothes laid out and you're already out the door. If he has one hobby, you have three. If he wants to take a trip with his buddies, you encourage him to go and then plan a trip for you and your girlfriends for the same time.

This shows him you're quick on your feet and one step ahead of him. You have a life outside of your life with him, which means he's in no danger of feeling smothered. Suddenly, he's not happy chilling on the sofa while you're out doing things. Yes, you can spend time together chilling on the sofa, but don't make it an everyday thing.

In what other ways can you challenge him?

Be Less Intense

One or both of you may have intense jobs so be less intense when you're spending time together. Relax on your dates and chill. Keep the serious conversations for another time.

Don't be an open book.

Let him learn about you in bits and pieces. Allow him to be intrigued by you. Forty years into a marriage, women can keep their man challenged by continually growing!

Be Open-Minded

Don't go into a relationship with a list of *"I would never..."* ride a roller coaster, own a boat, go jet skiing, or whatever.

Be open to new experiences. This says you aren't too intense or closed off. You're flexible and ready to take some risks. He knows life with you will be an adventure and that's a great thing!

When He Zigs, You Zag

Don't allow a man to become bored in your relationship. Change things up occasionally to keep things interesting. Surprise him with new things you're interested in and by trying new things. He doesn't care if you come home with purple hair.

He just shakes his head and smiles. Then, he wonders what could possibly be next. He's anticipating it with excitement!

This is For You Too

Becoming a challenge for a guy is as good for you as it is for him. It keeps you in a mode of trying new things and pushing outside the box. You're in a continuous mode of personal growth and that's never a bad thing!

This isn't about changing who you are to please a man. This is about doing what comes naturally. You aren't the same woman you were five years ago, and in five years, you won't be the same woman you are today. All you're doing by injecting challenge and mystery into your relationship is putting conscious thought into it.

CHAPTER 33

Are You Ready to Meet Him?

Boy, if this isn't the question of the hour! It's time to set the criteria for meeting your ex again. This is your criteria – not his.

He will show signs that he's ready. If he doesn't, reach out to him. Be confident and strong, so you are prepared for the meeting.

Contact with Your Ex

Up until now, you have played aloof while rebuilding your confidence, and he has had time to miss you. You have both been alone except for some small talk.

Before you consider meeting him, you need to have:

- Sent the letter soon after the breakup
- Improved your confidence

- Executed the slip in/slip out method
- Given him time to miss you and lose his contempt and negative feelings about your relationship

He needs to:

- Show signs of interest through social media, directly, or through your friends and family; this is known as the shift
- Change his behavior from anger and contempt to acceptance and intrigue

A rough estimate of when to engage him in small talk is after a minimum of 2 weeks of no contact and after executing slip in/slip out. Give him time to get over the negative feelings he has and start missing you.

If you are still grieving, and/or one of you still holds contempt, this timeline will be longer.

The timeline for engaging with him excludes any contact you are required to have because you have children together or work together. This early contact is only about those topics. Your emotions stay out even if he tries to trigger them.

Are You Ready to Meet Him? Have You Reined in Your Emotions?

To successfully sit down and have a meaningful conversation about starting a new relationship, you can't still be a puddle of tears or a ball of anger. You don't know what this meeting will be like, so you need to be in control of your emotions so you can react properly to him.

You Have Made at Least a Few Positive Changes in Your Life

You have made a few positive changes by now and you should be feeling pretty good about yourself and those changes.

You're making those changes for you, but also to let him know you aren't sitting home wallowing over losing him.

You are Absolutely Certain He's Worthy of You - This is a Good Decision

You have honestly assessed his personality, his ability to love and his mental health and he comes out on the positive side of those assessments.

You can't control him, and you don't want to. You also can't change him, so you must look at him as he is, or as he was when you broke up. If you did a good job of taking him off his pedestal, you have seen him for who he truly is.

You deserve a wonderful caring man who can love you for who you are. You do not deserve a man who will mistreat you in any way. This applies to your ex or any other man you date. This may be a good time to revisit the relationship deal breakers at the beginning of the book.

You've Been on at Least One Date

You may keep overlooking this part of Step Three out of fear, but to really sit down and have a meaningful meeting with your ex, you need to do this. You aren't betraying him. He's also dating – don't forget that!

You aren't together right now, so dating other men is not a betrayal. It doesn't make you loose, or anything else like that. It only makes you human.

Think of dating other men like trying on shoes. When you go to the shoe store, you try on different sizes, colors, and styles of shoes before you settle on one. Dating other men is the same thing. You're trying different personalities, looks and other traits on for size to see what you truly like.

You Can Pass This Test Without Falling Apart

Imagine you're meeting your ex for the first time since your breakup. He sits down and tells you he has met a great woman and he wants to pursue that relationship. He doesn't want a reconciliation with you.

How does that make you feel?

Prepare yourself for this possibility and know you can handle this news with grace and the ability to wish him well. If thinking of this possibility makes you fall apart, you aren't quite ready yet. Give yourself a little more time.

There is no point rushing this process. You're better off taking more time until you can stand to hear this news.

Is this the news you expect to hear? No, especially if you're executing the things you're learning in this book. However, you need to be prepared for all possible outcomes.

You Know You'll Be Okay No Matter What

If he does say he doesn't want to reconcile for one reason or another, you must know you'll be okay with the news. You are a confident woman who has a vision for her life and is creating a great story!

You are already dating, so you know other men are interested in you. Your ex isn't the only man who will date you. You have plenty of opportunities to find love with a great man who will treat you well.

Furthermore, this still doesn't mean it's over. Many men come limping back six months to a year later. Take solace in this fact. Yes, you will be deep into a new, exciting relationship but you will be able to relish in his loss!

You Have Used the Slip In/Slip Out Method at Least Once

The slip in/slip out method is useful for tweaking his good memories of you and your relationship, so do this at least once to remind him of what he's losing. It will help him overwrite his negative emotions about you and your relationship with those positive memories. He needs to miss you, even if just a little.

CHAPTER 34

Should You Contact Him?

If things go as planned, he will contact you.

Your response depends on his behavior and your level of confidence.

If your confidence is still low, buy more time until you are stronger. Tell him you are busy and will contact him later. Then, get back to your confidence building exercises! He needs to see you strong and happy. If he doesn't, he may reject you and this is detrimental to your cause.

Regardless of your confidence, contact him using the 'slip in/slip out' method.

You can handle slip in/slip out contact because it targets him in a different capacity than contacting him to say hi or to set up a meeting. The slip in/slip out tactic works best soon after the letter, but it can still be used later also.

For now, these are the only ways you should use to contact him. It's not time to call him on the phone and tell him how much you've missed him. That's a low confidence move and that isn't who you are any longer!

CHAPTER 35

The Shift

As you proceed through the steps, you are gathering intel on your ex. You're looking for the moment when he reaches out, or the shift.

If he is capable of love and you have enough great memories together, he will reach out.

It might occur next week, or it might happen in two years. There's no way to know. He risks losing you entirely if he waits too long. Some men figure this out while others stubbornly continue.

When the shift occurs, you've fully regained the power position. This is a time when ultimatums work and he's ready to talk with you about the relationship.

Examples of the shift:

- He texts you out of the blue

- He asks if you want to get together
- He contacts your friend to see how you are doing
- He takes interest in you again

When he reaches out, you can be honest about where you are in your life and your dating journey. Share what you're up to and how you feel about a possible reconciliation.

He's all ears!

You are responsible for this weak moment. It comes from everything you've done, from no contact to the letter to slip in/slip out; it's also come from building your confidence and dating other men.

If you used angry texts, begging and tear-filled voicemails, he'd be long gone, but since you've moved forward in a positive way, he's intrigued, challenged, and interested.

The shift doesn't mean he's changed or is ready to come back, so don't be fooled. He may be testing you to see if you're still his beck-and-call girl, which, of course, you **are not**.

Your current goal isn't reconciliation. You're listening to him and assuming the power position in the breakup. I know you're excited by his contact, but don't let your emotions drown out the logical process you've learned so far. Keep your wits about you and understand that he's not back, yet.

If he doesn't show signs of the shift, continue to occasionally use slip in/slip out without any mention of a reconciliation. You're just a friend reaching out.

This disarms him and opens a new line of communication.

While you're still hoping to reconcile with him, you need to set a timetable for his return. You should not sit around and wait for him indefinitely. He might not experience the shift for two years, and you shouldn't sit around and wait that long! Decide how long you're willing to wait before you get more serious about dating other men.

He runs the risk of you falling in love with another guy and he knows it.

CHAPTER 36

Are You Ready for Step 5?

Congratulations! You are about to begin Step Five! That is awesome and you should be proud of the work you've done so far!

How do you know when you're ready for Step Five?

You're ready for Step Five if:

- You've reined in your emotions
- You've assessed the breakup
- You're building your confidence steadily and regularly
- You've used No contact for at least two weeks
- You've sent him the letter
- You've used slip in/slip out a few times
- You can handle the possibility of him saying he doesn't want a reconciliation
- You've dated other men

step 5

Plan to Meet Him

WOW! It's time to plan to meet your ex. You might not be the one who suggests a meeting. He may suggest it first, and if he doesn't, you can get him to.

Make sure you've assessed whether you're ready to meet. If you're afraid to read the last chapter, it probably means you know you aren't ready, but you have anxiety about waiting too much longer to meet him.

If you meet him too soon, it won't end the way you want it to. You may get back together for a little while, but it won't last. It's worth taking the extra time now to make sure you're ready!

Prepare the acknowledgment of your role in the breakup. Even if your role was minor, this will disarm him and make him think.

He fully expects you to come into this meeting ranting and raving about how unfair the breakup was and what an awful person he is; or he may expect you to have teary apology for the entire mess and beg him back. Instead, you'll be sweet and serene with your acknowledgment in hand.

You're mysterious and challenging to him after your Step Four activities, but that won't stop him from being a little skeptical. He may test you by pushing old hot buttons but you're ready for that too.

In this final step, you will:

- Learn what he's thinking and feeling
- Acknowledge your role in the breakup
- Prepare for the worst
- Prepare for the tests he will try
- Know what you should and shouldn't discuss
- Understand why it's important that he chases you and how to make that happen
- Learn how to stay out of the friends with benefits zone
- Determine how you will move forward, either with or without him

CHAPTER 37

Casually Hanging Out with Your Ex

The first time you hang out with your ex, make it a casual meeting. Your goal is to establish if you can get together as friends, which is essential if you are going to reconcile and begin a new relationship.

This might come after he experiences the shift. You aren't thinking about getting back together with him. He might not be ready. This is just a chance to meet and have a friendly conversation.

After the shift, you will engage in casual conversation, and a meeting is a natural outcome of that conversation.

Don't call this a date because it isn't a date. This is two people hanging out to see if they can be friends. You know you have changed in the last few weeks, but you don't know about him. He might have changed, but that doesn't mean he changed for the better or that he's over the negativity of the breakup just yet.

Since it's not a date, don't make it dinner or drinks. Meet at a local coffee house or sit in the park. This is low-key, not high intensity. Go somewhere that feels relaxed and comfortable.

You Set the Time and Date

After your ex experiences the shift, he will ask for a meeting. You hold the power so plan the date and place. This tells him you aren't at his beck and call any longer. You're a busy woman who isn't sitting around waiting for him. You aren't eagerly anticipating any tiny scrap he throws your direction.

Your time is valuable. You're a busy woman and if he wants to rank high enough to get time on your schedule, he's needs to earn it! This won't push him away unless he still has low confidence and contempt, in which case, he's not ready to meet with you and you just saved yourself some time and energy.

Be Prepared

He might only want a hookup. That's a big no. It tells you where he stands with you now. If he only wants sex from you, stand firm and keep the meeting casual and in a public place. Don't go to his place or let him come to yours. It's too easy to give in.

Meeting with him may cause a rush of emotions, positive or negative, depending on how he acts. If he's all lovey-dovey, you may feel an instant attraction and heat. Prepare yourself for it so you can set aside those emotions and focus on his intentions.

If you feel some remaining anger and resentment, curtail your attitude. If you want him back, you can't show him this side of you, or he will retreat again. He doesn't want to hear how upset you are with him. He's hoping you've moved past that, or he wouldn't have reached out. Based on your actions, he believes you're happy and living a great life.

Remember, You're Starting Over

As you advance toward hanging out and making plans with your ex, understand that you are starting over. Any relationship you form from now forward is not a continuation of the old one. It's a brand-new relationship. You have kissed the old relationship goodbye. It was broken anyway so good riddance!

Since you're building a new relationship, the first few times you get together, you should avoid sex and serious talk about a committed relationship. One or both of you might be dating other people. **That is okay**. You do not have a commitment to one another any longer, so you aren't exclusive.

Rebuild the good experiences and trust that may have eroded or been forgotten in the aftermath of your breakup. He's moved past some of those negative vibes, but if you slip up and act clingy or needy, you will set the whole thing back.

A great relationship is built upon a foundation of good communication, trust, and friendship. While the two of you have history, it isn't all good history, so why try to drag it into this new relationship?

Cultivating a good relationship takes time. Anytime you hang out make sure it includes fun and reintroducing yourselves. You have changed and he has too. Get to know these new versions of yourselves. Remember in the beginning of this book when I said you needed to have good memories together to be able to reconcile?

When you start casually hanging out, you are building more memories together. Try new things together. Build new memories. The old memories are fine, but now it's time for some new ones.

Let Him See the New You... in Bits and Pieces

Don't forget about mystery and challenge as you consider hanging out. You're a new woman and he doesn't know you like he did before. You have new hobbies, friends, and new routines that he isn't aware of.

Mention how you started weightlifting at the gym and how well it's been going. Share your new hobby and tell him a little about it.

But spill these things in bits and pieces. He doesn't need the entire story in one sitting. Give him parts of chapters each time you meet. Inundating him with all the changes you've made might scare him a little, so ease him into it. If you have a new hairstyle or you've lost a few pounds, that might be all you need to reveal when you first meet.

You might feel that old infatuation, but you control your emotions now, and this is one time when you need to do so. Stay in public and avoid alcohol or anything else that may impair your judgment. Have daytime meetings where there is a lower chance of ending up in bed together.

Your biggest challenge during this time is not to get friend zoned.

Let Him Do Most of the Talking

This first meeting is a listening session for the most part. He is skeptical and isn't sure whether the changes he's heard about are real. You are skeptical of him too. Keep things fun and remain aloof over getting back together. That isn't your goal right now. You're just hanging out.

CHAPTER 38

What He'll Be Thinking and Feeling

What is your ex thinking and feeling? There are several possibilities with different outcomes.

WOW! Look at Her!

His first reaction might be holy cow, she really has been working out. Joe was right! This might catch him off guard for a second, but he'll recover. This is a good reaction, but he might backtrack just as quickly and wonder if your outward appearance is the only change.

Has She Really Changed?

Of course, he will wonder this. It's a natural question to ask and you will be asking yourself the same question about him.

He will wonder if your changes are cosmetic and temporary or if they run deeper and are more permanent. A lot of this will depend on how much he's seen and heard for himself versus what he's heard from friends.

Why Did I Break Up with Her?

He's been asking himself why he broke up with you for a little while, ever since he heard you've been making positive changes.

That's good, but it doesn't mean he's ready to get back together. It just means he likes what he's seen and heard, and he's intrigued. This isn't the time to let your guard down or slide backward in the progress you've made.

I Wonder if She'll be Okay with a Friends-with-Benefits Deal?

He might want casual hookups, but not a real relationship. He may miss having sex with you, but he either isn't ready to get back together or doesn't want to.

I doubt this is your motivation, but you are the only one who can truly answer this question. If all he wants is sex, he probably doesn't want anything long term.

How Will She React When I Tell Her I'm Not Coming Back?

He may not want to reconcile for a variety of reasons, or so he thinks right now. If he's found someone new, he probably wants to pursue that relationship. He may not be over all the negativity yet and isn't ready to jump back into what he still views as a negative situation.

He will be worried about your reaction, but you have prepared yourself for this possibility, so you'll handle it much better than he imagines.

I Just Want to Stay Friends with Her

He may just want friendship. It's certainly okay to have a friendship with an ex, but you need to decide if you can settle for that now.

Don't think that he will change his mind and want to get back into a committed relationship yet. Maybe he will, but don't hedge your bets on it. He might have another woman in the wings, and miss having you as his friend.

Watch His Body Language

His body language will tell you more than his words. Here are some body language cues to watch out for.

He's Sporting a Genuine Smile

You are familiar with is facial expressions, and you'll know if his smile is genuine or forced. If he is wearing a genuine smile, he's truly happy to see you and this is a good sign. If you're not sure, look for a smile that lights up his whole face. Can you catch the twinkle in his eye? If he has little crinkles out the outsides of his eyes, it's the real deal!

If he's frowning, he might not want anything to do with you. Frowning indicates disagreement with what you're saying or doing. If he's frowning, don't be afraid to ask him why.

His Posture is Open

Standing or sitting with arms crossed over your chest is closed body language while standing with hands down or arms wide is an open posture. This posture may mean he doesn't know how to feel or what to think. He is super nervous and anxious, closing himself off in a protective move.

An open body posture means he's not feeling defensive. He's feeling positive and open. He isn't worried about how this meeting will go.

His Body is Squared Toward You

We naturally point our bodies to the most important thing in the room. If he turns his body so his shoulders are squared and facing you, he's indicating you're important to him. If he stays turned away from you, this isn't the case.

He Leans in When You Talk

Someone who is interested in what you have to say leans toward you as a gesture that he's interested in what you're saying. He's engaged in the conversation and he's listening intently to what you have to say.

If he's pulling back, he's disengaged and disinterested. He is trying to create some physical distance between you.

He Avoids Eye Contact

If he won't make eye contact with you, there could be an innocent reason, but you'll know right away. If your guy is shy, he might not make eye contact. Otherwise, he's disinterested, he's avoiding you, or he's in denial. If he maintains good eye contact, he's happy in the conversation and things are going well!

Is He Fidgety?

Does he touch his hair or fidget with his hands? Putting his hands through his hair a few times is a sign of attraction. This is also true if he's touching other parts of his body like ears. He's thinking about you, even when you're not together.

If you know him well, and you know that this is a nervous habit for him, then that's all it is and there is no hidden meaning behind it, but if this hand in hair thing is new, you're in good shape!

Look at His Feet

When your ex points his toes directly toward you, it's a sign of affection. He is still interested in you or at least he's willing to talk and engage in a friendly conversation!

If he's shaking his leg or feet, he's nervous, impatient and/or ready to move on to something else. If he's tapping his foot, he's moments away from leaving. He wants out.

If his feet or legs are uneasy, so is he. Don't force any conversations. Instead, slide into talking about something that might help him relax. He might want you back and he's nervous about how this meeting will go. If he relaxes and talks about something he enjoys and he's interested in getting back or continuing the conversation, the nervousness will subside.

If his feet touch you, he's very attracted to you. He is eager to be with you!

Which Way are His Feet and Knees Pointing?

This can be a bigger tell-tale sign than any smile or facial expression. If he turns his legs and feet away from you, it might mean he doesn't want to talk to you.

If his feet are planted on the floor solidly, he's either showing or trying to show you that he's confident.

He Kisses You on the Cheek

When a new guy you've never kissed kisses you on the cheek, he's testing the waters to see how you'll respond. He's looking for a little encouragement. But when your ex kisses you on the cheek, it means that in that moment, he felt something.

It does not necessarily mean he wants to get back together, but it means something stirred inside him.

He Hugs You

Don't read too much into a hug. It might just be a friendship hug and not indicative of something romantic. Let's examine the difference.

A friendly hug is short and a little stiff. You can call it a half-hug. You wrap your arms around someone's shoulders, tap off a little hug and pull back.

But just because he hugged you this way doesn't mean he isn't interested. It could mean he's nervous as heck and not sure how well his hug will be received. Look for other cues.

A more passionate hug is longer and has a little more umph to it. He squeezes you a little or uses his hands to rub circles or pat your back. This type of hug makes you feel a little weak in the knees and it was probably preceded with him gazing into your eyes, even if momentarily.

Even if he gives you a passionate hug, it doesn't mean he wants to get back together. It simply means he has strong feelings toward you.

He's Gained Weight

If it's only been a few weeks since your breakup and your ex has gained some weight, it could be a sign of depression. Many people eat their way through depression. He discovered that his life without you in it isn't what he imagined.

It could also mean that he's having difficulty dealing with the heavy emotions of the breakup that he didn't anticipate.

He Mimics Your Gestures & Positioning

When someone mimics or mirrors your body language, it's a strong positive sign that he still has feelings for you.

Test him out. Move an arm or cross your legs. Lean in or lean away and see if he mirrors your movements. He might not realize he's doing it.

CHAPTER 39

Acknowledge Your Role in the Breakup

When you meet with your ex, things will be tense at first. There are probably unspoken things between you because you didn't part company on the best terms and things may have been said that one or both of you now regret.

Previously, you prepared to acknowledge your role in the breakup, and you assessed what that might be. You've had time to deal with this knowledge and make any course corrections.

If you owe an apology, there is no shame in delivering it. What you should be prepared to do, however, is to acknowledge your role. This is a bit disarming because he expects you to blame him for everything.

Be genuine and honest; speak from the heart and be genuinely sorry for your role. With any luck, this will prompt him to acknowledge his own role in the breakup and you're off to a great start.

Some things you might say include:

- Jim, I know in the past you may have felt as if I didn't pay enough attention to you, and I want you to know I see that now and it's something I'm working on
- Gregg, I didn't realize until a few weeks ago how negative I had become, and I know it had a negative impact on our relationship; that phase in my life is gone and I am happy again
- Steve, I recognize now that I was holding you back from spending time with your friends and doing things without me; I'm okay with it now

Acknowledge what you see as your role and the impact it may have had on him. Share that you've made positive changes to avoid the problem in the future.

It might take him a moment or two to respond and his body language may change for a few minutes while he processes this new information.

You're challenging him and he needs a minute to process that and respond accordingly. The challenge part is a good thing! What he does with the information remains to be seen.

This can open a conversation about your relationship and that isn't necessarily your goal. A conversation like that could quickly downgrade to an argument. Decide if the two of you can go there at this juncture.

If he slides into a conversation about your past relationship and you are not ready for it, shift the conversation in a new direction.

"Oh, enough about our past. Tell me what you've been doing lately? How did that big project at work come out?"

Keep things upbeat and friendly. Acknowledging your role in the breakup is an important step, but it doesn't mean you should spend the whole time rehashing old stuff.

Let that stuff go. The purpose in acknowledging your role in the breakup is to disarm him and let him know you've changed, but your words won't be enough, just like his words won't be enough for you. He is looking to your actions to prove to himself that you've truly changed.

CHAPTER 40

Prepare for the Worst

It's possible that he doesn't want to reconcile, regardless of how much work you've put into improving yourself or how well you deliver your acknowledgment of your role in the breakup.

He might be happier with his life as it is right now.

Most men won't meet with you to have this conversation. They will just text or disappear.

Regardless, prepare yourself for this possibility. No matter how many times you read it, I know it will still come as a sucker punch in the gut.

If this is the outcome of your meeting, remember you've already dated other men. He isn't the only man in the world, and he certainly isn't the only one who will love you.

Heck, he might not even deserve you! It depends on how much work he did on himself during your breakup. If he spent the entire time avoiding his emotions and rebound dating, you aren't in the same.

Sometime in the future, he may realize he's made a mistake, but how long are you willing to wait? How long will you sit by and avoid finding a great man who deserves you?

Not long!

As you build your confidence, different men will appeal to you. Confident men. And you will appeal to them.

Confidence is something you can see in another person's body language. They look you in the eye. They walk with their head up and their shoulders squared, not hunched over. They don't hide behind hair or sunglasses. Their body language is open.

This is how men know you're a confident woman as well. The more your confidence builds, the more natural this will become.

Set a time limit for how long you'll put your life on hold to wait for him. Great men will come around, but if you wait too long for something that may not happen, you'll miss out on some great opportunities to meet wonderful men.

Even if you decide to wait for him for a while, continue to date other men. There is **nothing** wrong with dating other men until you are in a committed relationship, which you are not currently. Right now, you two are broken up. There is no commitment to your ex at all. He broke that commitment when he broke up with you.

CHAPTER 41

Be Ready Because He Will Test You

Assume you and your ex set up a meeting. This is not a date so don't call it a date. It is a meeting the two of you have agreed upon to see if you want to try a new relationship.

Notice that wording – a new relationship. Anything you and your ex do from now forward is a **new** relationship. It is **not** a continuation of your previous relationship.

Why?

That relationship was broken. Why would you want to continue it? It ended; therefore you can't continue it.

He'll be skeptical. He's seen and/or heard about the new you, but he hasn't seen or heard enough of it directly from you to believe it's true.

Acknowledging your role in the breakup won't make him a believer, and it isn't your job to spend this meeting convincing him otherwise.

This is his meeting. Your job is to be aloof and an excellent listener.

Prepare yourself for him to test you and push hot buttons. Don't react, no matter how much you want to. You're no longer reactive. You think about your reactions before you deliver them. Remember that!

He might attempt to trigger some sort of anger from you. Don't let him. It's all a test to see if you've truly changed.

Meanwhile, evaluate his body language and assess where he's coming from. Is his body language open? Is he smiling with his eyes in a genuine smile? Is he looking you in the eye? Remember those positive cues and watch for them.

He might bring old issues he still thinks he needs to resolve. Since you delivered your acknowledgment and maybe an apology, there is no need to rehash old business.

He's trying to get under your skin. If he continues to proceed in a negative way, he isn't ready for or interested in a reconciliation. He needs more time to get over negativity. He hasn't changed enough yet.

Some more dos and don'ts:

- Do let him be the one to do most of the talking

- Don't bring up your old relationship or start playing the blame game
- Do avoid his traps to make you angry, frustrated, or sad
- Do be prepared to stand up and walk out if he continues to exhibit anger or frustration
- Do not agree to any reconciliation at this meeting
- Do have a list of your own of things that you require out of a new relationship, in case the conversation is productive and not antagonistic
- Do not allow him to attempt to abuse you in any way
- Don't have sex with him
- **Do show him that you will thrive with or without him!**

You need to rebuild trust in one another. It's most likely broken, due to the nature of a breakup. He doesn't trust this new you and you shouldn't automatically trust him until he has earned it back. Allow him the opportunity to regain your trust. Don't make it so difficult for him to earn your trust back that he can't ever get there.

A new relationship with your ex is just that. You don't pick up where you left off, sleeping, or even living together, no matter how convenient and economical it is. Learn to be friends again. Learn to trust one another again. Build it slowly and steadily.

CHAPTER 42

Gather Intel

The meeting will provide useful information so use it to your benefit.

After a few fun moments of reminiscing, he may indicate that he wants to get back together. Be careful and don't allow your excitement to get the better of you. It's okay to tell him you need to think about it.

Then, do just that! Think about things! Talk to yourself, your friends, and your family. Take a few days. If you are ready to give your relationship a second chance, set up a trial period and evaluate things again after it has ended.

You are the boss now. **You** are allowing him back into your life, not the other way around.

If your ex is a wishy-washy mess, tell him you need to go and continue with the steps above. Make sure you have an expiration date on how long you're willing to wait for him to come back to you.

Pay attention to his actions more than his words. Remember those body language signals and be aware of what his body is telling you, not his mouth. Men will say anything to a woman if they think it will make her happy and your ex is no different, but what he says aloud versus what his body language is signaling, probably without him realizing it, may be two very different things!

CHAPTER 43

How to Stay Out of the Friends-with-Benefits Zone

If you decide to start a new relationship with your ex, there are a few things you need to do to stay out of the friend zone.

If you want a reconciliation and he only wants to be friends, you need to reject his friendship offer for now. At some point, you can attempt a friends-only arrangement, but when one of you wants one thing and the other doesn't, the best thing is to cut the cord completely.

This is his attempt to keep you in his life while he dates other women. Nothing has changed for him. It's the same old crap. He wants you for his beck-and-call girl and nothing more.

If you agree you want to enter a relationship again, starting as friends is the best plan. The trick is to avoid entering the friend zone, or even worse, the friends with benefits zone.

What's the difference?

The friends with benefits zone means you sleep together. Period. Maybe you hang out a little, but your relationship is mostly sexual. I doubt this is what you're looking for and he can find that on Tinder.

The friend zone is a relationship where one of you has unreciprocated feelings toward the other. In other words, you want a relationship, and he wants a friendship, just as described above.

How to Stay out of the Friends-with-Benefits Zone

No matter how much you want to feel him against you and be back to your old relationship status of sleeping together, don't.

I know you still want him back, but if he's friend-zoning you, it means he doesn't want this either, but he does want an easy hookup.

You deserve much more than that!

And that's exactly what you tell him, *"I'm sorry Jack, but I deserve a man who isn't just into me for sex."*

It might feel as if you're getting him back, but you aren't. He's only in it for the sex and eventually, he will find someone he wants to be in a relationship with and it most likely won't be you. Cut your losses now. You're already broken up. Leave it that way!

How to Stay out of the Friend Zone

Walk Away

The first step in staying out of the friend zone is to be willing to walk away. If you're hanging out together but he doesn't seem to be interested in treating it more like a date, head on out the door. Go meet up with some friends. Talk to others where you are or just go home and enjoy what's left of the day or evening. If he isn't showing interest in you, it's time to move on. If you walk away and he realizes he wants to spend time with you, he'll do a better job of showing it next time.

Continue Dating Other Men

Continue dating other men. If he wants to engage in a new relationship with you and he wants to get on your dating radar, he knows he needs to step up his game. His lame attempts so far aren't going to cut it.

Stay Busy

Continue pursuing your hobbies, volunteering, and hanging out with your friends. When he calls, thinking he can ask you out last minute for pizza and a beer, you're busy. You are not his beck and call girl. Let that be someone else.

Kindly decline his invitation and suggest another option, *"I'm sorry Tony but I'm busy tonight. How about we check out the new pizza place downtown next Tuesday.*" If he wants to get onto your schedule, he'll work harder at it.

Withhold Your Responses

When he texts you, unless it's for an immediate date request as previously mentioned, withhold your response for at least twenty minutes up to a couple hours or maybe even the next morning.

Men don't text back right away, and he doesn't expect a response from you right away either. He won't see it or reply immediately anyway. It's okay to do this. It doesn't show disinterest on your part. It is you acting like one of his guy friends and challenging him by doing something he doesn't expect.

Don't Be Subtle

If you two haven't officially had a "let's get back together" conversation, it's time. Let him know what you want from your renewed friendship. Be clear about exactly what you want.

Remember, you hold the power now!

Do not fear of the outcome. Wouldn't you like to know sooner rather than later? Why spend weeks or longer with someone who only wants you as a friend?

Touch Him

There is a lot of power in physical touch, especially if you have sexual history together. The act of touching his arm gently or brushing your hand across his as you reach for the nachos is subtle and sends a strong message. It's okay to give him a hello or goodbye kiss on the cheek.

If you can do it and it doesn't seem awkward, rest your head on his shoulder. If he responds by putting his arm around your back, you're working your way out of the friend zone. If you're still sitting like that thirty minutes later, you've probably exited or avoided the friend zone.

In the case of the first meeting, touching him doesn't mean you're taking him back. You are here to listen. Go home and tell him you will think about the things he said and get back to him.

Touch him and get up to leave because you have plans… BAM!

Statements that Let You Know You're in the Friend Zone

- I wish I could meet someone like you, you're such a great friend
- Let's invite a few friends to hang out at Rude Dog this weekend
- Hey, I'm super busy right now, can I call you back later (with no return call later)
- You're such a great person! Why do you think I made you my friend?
- I went out with this girl last night and I just don't understand why she….

Behaviors that Let You Know You're in the Friend Zone

- One-sided conversations where you find yourself trying to keep it going
- Regularly pointing out other women's attractiveness
- Referring to you as his friend

CHAPTER 44

What If He Doesn't Experience the Shift and Doesn't Plan a Meeting?

You've done all the work, but he still hasn't come around. All your work has improved your life, so you are in a strong position to start not giving a crap about him.

This will happen over time - I guarantee it. Time is an amazing cure for someone who wants to act like you don't matter.

Contact Him

Let's imagine he hasn't contacted you for a month or two. What do you do?

Say hi to him out of the blue.

It's okay, you can handle however he reacts even if he doesn't react at all. You are strong and you should be dating other men. You have options.

Send him a fun text that he will like. A pic, an article, or a video about a hobby he is into. Keep it short and pithy.

> *"Jim! How the heck is my ex doing? Hey, felt the need to send you this YouTube video – I knew you would get a laugh from it! Hope you are doing well."*
>
> *Jesse*

This message is very disarming. There is no pressure. It's upbeat and you even kid him about being your ex. He feels no pressure. This becomes the perfect setup for him to respond.

He may be afraid of being rejected or feel ashamed for failing you, your friends, and your family. His low self-esteem might keep him from loving you because he doesn't love himself.

There are many reasons why he didn't experience the shift and they don't involve you. You don't know so send him a fun text.

If there's still no response, wait three months and do it again, if you haven't found someone else. Guys almost always have weak moments and it's all about timing, so keep the communication corridor open every now and then, if you feel the desire to do so.

CHAPTER 45

How to Move Forward

There are two obvious move-forward scenarios – with him and without him.

Moving Forward with Him

This is the holy grail! You've reached your goal of getting him back! Congratulations! My sincerest hope for you is a lifetime of happiness.

Treat this as a new relationship. Learn to like one another again. Work on building trust and great memories together. Slowly ease back into this new relationship.

Just because you've both agreed to try again doesn't mean it will work. A lot will depend on how well this new you meshes with whatever version of him you're seeing now. Decide between you that this is a trial arrangement for now. This keeps expectations where they should be and avoids major disappointment if things don't work out.

After the trial period, if things still seem okay and you don't feel as though you've been friend zoned, or worse friends with benefits zoned, begin to move things forward.

While you're in the trial period, discuss if it's okay to date other people. Your relationship is new, and you have no commitment to one another yet. This can be touchy so talk about it.

Visit my other website, **WhoHoldstheCardsNow.com** and focus on reading the Find a Guy articles (whoholdsthecardsnow.com/i-want-to-find-a-guy), as well as the Understanding Men articles (whoholdsthecardsnow.com/understand-men).

Moving Forward without Him

If you've decided not to take him back or he doesn't want a relationship with you right now, you're moving forward without him. This doesn't take away from the great work you did throughout this book.

All that work prepared you for a relationship with a new guy. Your ex may change his mind somewhere down the line, but every day that he waits, he risks losing you forever. He knows that but he still seems to be willing to take the chance.

Visit my other website, **WhoHoldstheCardsNow.com** and focus on reading the Keep a Guy articles (whoholdsthecardsnow.com/i-want-to-keep-my-guy), as well as the Understanding Men articles (whoholdsthecardsnow.com/understand-men).

Wrap Up

Congratulations on reaching the end of your journey! One way or the other, you are all set for a new, fulfilling, and successful relationship. I hope you get the relationship you seek, whether it's with your ex or another guy.

I've mentioned my other website, Who Holds the Cards Now? a couple of times in the book already, but there's one more area of that site I want to let you know about. It's the **Build Yourself area**.

Visit this area, regardless of your current situation with your ex. Confidence takes a hit throughout your life and it's imperative to have a great confidence-building tool set to help you through!

You did some great work throughout this book! You learned how to control your emotions and you're working on using your wise mind, instead of your emotional mind. You have boundaries and you're nobody's doormat! You aren't experiencing the stages of mourning your relationship as much, although you may find yourself in one for a brief time every now and then.

You assessed your relationship with your ex, and you have a firm grasp on what went wrong, whether it was your fault or that of your ex. This will help you build a better, stronger relationship in the future. You have a much better idea of what you will and will not tolerate in future relationships!

Then, you took the big step and built your independence. Your next relationship will be an interdependent relationship! You made positive changes in your life and changed your routines. Keep up the good work! You have a self-care routine and you've got it regularly scheduled. You have a vision and you're writing one heck of a great story. And finally, you're no victim! You're a student of life, soaking it all up and wanting more!

You got a small lesson in understanding men in the last two steps. You can carry this information forward as you move on, with or without your ex. You know how to stay out of the friend zone and are in no danger of becoming friends with benefits.

You're about to enter a new chapter of your life and I'm excited for you! Browse through the recommended reading. You've graduated from being in ex back mode to being a woman on the prowl! Go get 'em!

Recommended Reading

You're Moving on Without Your Ex

Riding Solo

Unleashing the Tigress Within

He's Gone Now What

To Date a Man, You Must Understand a Man

The Untold Secrets of What Men Want

Weed Out the Losers, the Couch Potatoes and the Users

The Little Self-Care Handbook

Own Your Tomorrow

You're Moving on With Your Ex

Pennies in the Jar: How to Keep a Man for Life

Who Holds the Cards Now?

To Date a Man, You Must Understand a Man

The Untold Secrets of What Men Want

The Little Self-Care Handbook

Own Your Tomorrow

Find All My Books Here

WhoHoldstheCardsNow.com

Author Bio

As one of Boston's top dating coaches, my books rest prominently atop the dating advice genre. In my role as a life coach, I've been known to be unorthodox, in a good way, and I break a few rules. I assist both men and women and help them understand one another.

I won't bore you with my professional bio. Instead, I will share with you the story of how I became a dating and life coach and what makes me qualified to coach you.

The irony of my story is that I come from an extremely dysfunctional family. I witnessed the marriage of my parents crumble before my eyes at an early age. Flying dishes seemed normal in my household. I came out a bit angry and I have 12 years of failed relationships to show for it.

Fortunately, I started encountering positive things in my life. I discovered that couple, that elusive, elderly couple still holding hands in the park at the ripe old age of eighty. They gave me hope. As a problem solver, I could solve anything…except relationships, darn it!

I couldn't figure out why my folks represented the norm rather than the exception to married life. Fifty-five percent of all marriages end in divorce. Why? What is wrong?

In 2009, after a long stretch of living the single life, I had an epiphany. I attended a Christmas show at my Dad's church. I am not a religious person, but when I saw the cheerful couples and witnessed the powerful music, I was touched. I needed answers to love and I wanted true love for myself.

I was tired of my shallow single life. I decided to study my failures and interview as many single people and couples as I could. I even watched the movie, Hitch, and it motivated me to help others.

I realized I possessed a natural ability to help others discover love, and knew it was my future. Can you guess where I started? Yep, those happy elderly couples. Sure, I got maced a few times as I approached them with questions, but the knowledge I gained was priceless!

Since then, I have met thousands of people: happy couples, unhappy couples, single people of all types, and everything in between. I quickly learned that confidence played a large role in both attracting and keeping a partner.

My friends encouraged me to launch a dating advice website. I now own the top dating site for women, **WhoHoldsthe CardsNow.com**.

Men and women contact me after reading my books. I have become a "Dear Abby" of sorts. Today, after thousands of interviews, I have accomplished my goal. I broke the code and enjoy a great relationship myself. Now I plan to share my findings with **you**!

I have come to realize that even though people believe what I teach, they still suffer a serious problem. They lack the motivation and confidence to execute my tactics. A course change was required. I started concentrating on life coaching in addition to my date coaching. If you can't love yourself, how can you love someone else? It's impossible.

Now, I concentrate on pulling people in and guiding them to understanding themselves. I assist them in creating clarity in their lives, setting goals, and creating the path to attain those goals. I offer inspiration, passion, and spirituality with the constant live like you're dying attitude. People are transformed through my books and daily exercises.

I have written numerous Amazon Best Sellers, several of which reached #1 Best Seller status. Together we can build your confidence, increase your self-esteem, and propel you closer to your goals.

You will discover happiness by completing the work most people will never attempt!

Today, I travel and teach in all the sexy playgrounds: LA, South Beach, and Las Vegas. I can help you in your journey to find love and build confidence so we can transform your life.

I am not merely a best-selling author, my readers are my friends and I communicate with them directly. I humbly ask you to allow me to help you. Join me on my quest for your happiness, your exciting journey to an extraordinary life!

Gregg Michaelsen, Confidence Builder

Get the Word Out

If you believe your friends would draw something valuable from this book, I'd be honored if you'd share your thoughts with them. If you feel strongly about the contributions this made to your success getting him back, I'd be eternally grateful if you would post a review on Amazon.

Printed in Great Britain
by Amazon

17016271R00197